MW00615218

# WHEELS UP

## Sky Jinks in the Jet Age

WHEELS UP: Sky Jinks in the Jet Age.

Copyright © 2014 by Steve Taylor.
All rights reserved. Printed in the United States of America. No part of
this book may be used or reproduced in any manner whatsoever without written permission except in the case of brief quotations embod-
ied in critical articles and reviews. For information, address Joggling
Board Press LLC, P.O. Box 13029, Charleston, South Carolina 29422.

Joggling Board Press books may be purchased for educational, business
or sales promotion use. For information, please contact
sales@jogglingboardpress.com.

FIRST EDITION
Edited by Susan Kammeraad-Campbell
with Jess Laughlin and Elizabeth Palmieri
Cover and interior design by Torborg Davern

Library of Congress Cataloging-in-Publication Data applied for.
ISBN-hardcover: 978-0-9914911-0-0
ISBN-trade paperback: 978-0-9914911-1-7

# CAPTAIN STEVE TAYLOR

# WHEELS UP

## Sky Jinks in the Jet Age

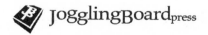

# ≡ CONTENTS ≡

*To my wife: Nancy T. Taylor*
*Partner, lover, critic*

# WHEELS UP

## Sky Jinks in the Jet Age

# ═ PROLOGUE ═

*I've always been different with one foot over the line*
*Winding up somewhere one step ahead or behind*
*It ain't been so easy but I guess I shouldn't complain*
*I've always been crazy but it's kept me from going insane.*

—WAYLON JENNINGS

Delta was taxiing out for takeoff. United had just landed and was on her way in. As they passed on the taxiway, Delta Captain McSwine shot the United captain the bird and, at the same time, picked up the phone and addressed the passengers. "Ladies and Gentlemen, off to your left you will see the friendly skies of United." They all looked in time to see the United airplane slowly taxi by while its captain, in plain view, returned Captain McSwine's insult.

Most airline pilots have a highly developed sense of humor. We are self-assured, professional and smart – a nice way of saying we're cocky. Some are also incorrigible practical jokers. It was my highest privilege to be included in this fun fraternity, and I did my best to be a worthy contributor.

My fascination with flying began when I was six years old, visiting a small airport with my father. It was all new to me, and I was utterly transfixed. The owner of a single-engine plane noticed my fascination and asked if I would like to go for a ride. *Would I!* My father hesitated. I begged. Reluctantly he allowed me to go. From his ground-level vantage, little did my dad know that his son's life was being changed forever.

Sometime after VJ Day, there was an exhibition at the Charleston Air Base. On display that day was a B-29, the biggest, most sophisticated airplane built in 1946. Already it was legendary – it had delivered "Little Boy," "Fat Man" and 200,000 tons of other bombs to defeat the Japanese. Entering the open bomb bay, I made my way through a tunnel to the cockpit. I feasted my eyes on a thousand dials, switches and levers, instantly consumed by the thought of mastering this machine.

By age 18, I had saved enough money to take my first flying lessons and so began my insatiable appetite for bigger, faster machines.

I was flying for the U.S. Air Force in Southeast Asia when I first heard talk about the appealing lifestyle of airline pilots: no extra duties, just flying, nobody bothering you, good pay and lots of time off. My first thought was it sounded too good to be true. But when I began working for Delta Air Lines, the reality of it turned out to be even better than I imagined. Not only was flying more pleasure than work, it was also a fine place for storytelling pranksters. Over the years, I have enjoyed being a participant in, and the butt of, many a good story. I first began thinking of writing them down when "Steve Taylor stories" came back to me greatly distorted. Although most all of the stories are connected to flying, not all are humorous. Some dip into the more dramatic and challenging moments of my life. Absurdism found its place during my time at The Citadel, in the military, with Delta and after retirement, but occasionally rationality actually dominated.

The stories I have compiled here are true to the best of my recollection and research. The people are real, though at times, I changed a name but never the character. Whenever possible, I have verified points with others who were there. Over time and through many tellings, some small detail may stray from the hard fact and setting , but the truth of the story is intact.

Flying so fit me, it is hard for me to imagine having done anything else. If I hadn't had to support my family I would have done my flying job with Delta for free. Nah, I would have paid them to let me do it.

A pilot who is good at his job must think he is good, for confidence goes with the job. Was I good? You bet I was. And on the day I was forced to retire due to age, I was the best I had ever been. My career in aviation spanned the best of times. This was the dawn of the jet age, and airlines were growing fast and making money. Airplanes were less crowded, flight attendants were young and pretty, and due to rapid expansion a new pilot could expect to spend much of his career as a captain. Airlines competed for well-trained military pilots. Delta had the finest reputation in the business. Their pilots were the highest paid in the industry, and equipment progression advanced rapidly. For most of my career, Delta passengers dressed like they were going out to Sunday dinner.

Imagine for a moment what it would be like to be the captain on a Delta jumbo jet preparing for a trip to Europe. You report an hour and a half before departure to familiarize yourself with all aspects of the trip and oversee the flight preparation. Your crew is so competent that hardly any instruction is necessary. Everyone is friendly and accommodating. If people know you, they address you by your first name. If not, by Captain.

You know that no two trips are alike and possibly there will be problems to solve, but this, too, is gratifying. Because of your experience, your training and your aptitude, not only are you confident you can handle any situation, but you look forward to the challenge. The passengers and other Delta staff treat you with respect and favor, and once the cabin door is shut, your authority is absolute.

Then the best part: there is a surge of adrenaline as you push the throttles forward and feel the power of the giant engines. As you accelerate through 150 miles per hour you gently pull half a million pounds of precision machinery and passengers off the ground, and, as always, you are slightly awed that it flies.

*Nancy and me beside Delta's Big Jet, Frankfurt, Germany.*

# PART 1

AN INTRODUCTORY AIRLINE STORY

# ≡ CHAPTER 1 ≡
## NO LANDING PILOT

*Oh, what a tangled web we weave,*
*when first we practice to deceive.*

—SIR WALTER SCOTT

*CV-880, a serious gas-guzzler, but then fuel was 11 cents a gallon.*

1970: HOUSTON, TEXAS — The Convair 880, a four-engine hotrod, was the queen of the sky. Narrow-bodied and fast, it only carried 96 passengers – on the first delivery flight to Delta it set an intercontinental speed record of 665 mph. But, with no fuel saving fans, the engines burned gas like a Maserati and blew black smoke out of the noisy exhaust. Coming or going, she was hard to miss.

For the month of November, I was scheduled to fly as co-pilot on the CV-880 with Captain Dick Caravella. This pleased me. Dick was a 20-year veteran of Delta. He had a spotless record and was an excellent captain. Graying temples and a pleasant commanding voice left no doubt of his captain's authority. On a previous flight, I watched how he handled a mechanic who resisted fixing a minor maintenance issue. The mechanic and I both felt that the delay we took was unnecessary and that it could wait until the plane was parked for a maintenance inspection. But Caravella explained his logic with such courtesy and professionalism that, by the time we left, we were thanking him for the good decision.

The flight engineer was Jake Armstrong, a young, athletic pilot who had been working at Delta for about 18 months. He was a graduate of the Naval Academy and had six years of navy flying with two tours in Vietnam. Jake was smart, laid back and, like Caravella, had a great sense of humor.

During the second day of our first trip together, we stopped in Dallas en route to Atlanta. The scheduled flight attendants could not make our flight, so reserve standbys were called in. Typically, standbys were newer employees. Because we were missing all of our flight attendants, the whole crew was new, straight from training.

The Federal Aviation Administration (FAA) had many requirements for flight attendants to learn about their particular job, but that training did not include much about what goes on in the cockpit. Trainees were taught that the captain was in command and that pilots were well trained and knew their job.

As we observed the new flight attendants rush about the plane in a semi-panic, Dick and I contemplated the great potential here for mischief. The opportunity presented itself when one of the girls serving first class finally had time to come forward and offer us something to drink.

"Hi, I'm Judy. I'm sorry I haven't been up, but we are all new and it's a little hectic."

We introduced ourselves, and she took our drink order. Dick winked at Jake and asked him to see if there was anyone in the lavatory. The first class lavatory on the Convair 880 was on the cabin side of the cockpit bulkhead, next to the engineer's panel. Close to the bulkhead was a small light on a swivel. Because the light was not on, to an unfamiliar eye, it was but one of a thousand mysterious dials and gadgets in the cockpit. Jake leaned over with his eye close to the lens and moved it around slightly. "No sir, it's empty right now."

Judy watched this carefully and with wide eyes exclaimed, "You can see in the bathroom?"

Dick explained, "Don't get upset – it's a safety requirement. We need to know if somebody is incapacitated in there, or if they are doing something they're not supposed to."

"Bu . . . but . . . I was just in there."

Jake, in a low voice, said, "Yes, I know."

Red-faced, Judy left and we weren't entirely sure she would return with our drinks. But in case she did, we quickly cooked up a half-baked plan to further test her gullibility quotient.

Soon enough she reappeared with our drinks. Dick gave me a quick glance then said to her, "Something has come up, and since you are the acting flight attendant leader, you should know about it."

On every flight, one person is designated the lead attendant or "A line." In this case, because they were all brand new, it may have been only a few days' seniority that caused Judy to be the A line.

Judy took in Captain Caravella's serious tone and her indignation quickly turned to concern.

"Is something wrong?" she asked.

"Yes, there is. Steve and I were wondering why we had never flown together before, and we realized that both of us are take-off pilots."

I honestly thought this was too absurd for her to buy, but Dick was so serious and dignified it was hard not to believe him.

"What does that mean?" she asked.

Dick continued, "We both have had extensive training in airplane take-off procedures, but neither of us has been trained to land. If a pilot is a take-off pilot he is forbidden by regulation to land the airplane. In the old days, pilots sometimes did both, but today we live in a specialized world."

"You can land it if you need to, can't you?" Judy looked very concerned.

"Well, I'm not sure. It's been a long time since I've landed one.

Steve, how long has it been since you've landed?"

"I have never landed one," I said, doing my best to sound serious. "I was trained as a take-off pilot when I first started with Delta."

"How could you be a pilot and never have landed an airplane?" she said.

"These airplanes are so complex," I said, "it would be almost impossible to stay proficient in both taking off and landing."

I wasn't sure if the wrinkle in her brow expressed anxiety or doubt.

Meanwhile, Dick stood and announced he was going to contact the company on the engineer's radio. At first I didn't follow what he was up to, but I suddenly realized what I needed to do. By leaving his seat, he triggered the high altitude oxygen regulation. Anytime a pilot left his flight position at high altitude the other pilot had to wear his oxygen mask. The mask covered the nose and mouth and had a microphone transmitter for talking over the intercom or on the radio, depending on the switch position. While wearing the mask, it would be impossible for others to see him talking.

Judy looked skeptical as Dick picked up the engineer's microphone and moved two or three switches. This subterfuge was to disguise him setting the microphone switch to intercom so that our conversation could only be heard in the cockpit. Meanwhile, I put on my oxygen mask and set my switch to intercom.

Dick keyed the engineer's mic and called, "Atlanta radio, Atlanta radio, this is Delta 482, over."

"This is Atlanta radio, go-ahead 482," I answered through my mask microphone.

"Atlanta, we have a serious problem. We need to talk to flight control."

"Roger 482, standby."

Judging from the size of her eyes, it was clear we had her on the hook again.

Speaking into the oxygen mask, I said, "Delta 482, this is flight control, go ahead."

"Roger, flight control," Dick answered. "We have just discovered that both pilots on this airplane are take-off pilots and there is no landing pilot onboard. Would you study our situation and please advise? Over."

"Delta 482, understand you do not have a landing pilot on board?"

"That's affirmative. We have no landing pilot on board."

"482, standby, we'll call you back."

Judy's knuckles turned white in the death grip she had on the jump-seat arm rest. "What are we going to do?" she exclaimed.

In a calm, professional tone, Dick comforted her. "Don't give up hope. We will try to work something out. As the lead flight attendant, you must be brave and calm."

While he was giving her this hokey speech, I was trying to decide what "flight control" was going to say.

"Delta 482, this is flight control, over."

"This is 482, go ahead flight control."

"Roger 482, we have researched your problem with technical operations, and it was discovered that your airplane is equipped with a new Mark 36-70 autopilot. This autopilot is capable of landing the airplane, but it is still in the experimental phase. The problem is that the autopilot goes into a take-off mode five minutes after landing. So far our technical people have not been able to prevent it. If you wish to use the autopilot, we will guide you through its operations, but you must be aware of the take-off mode five minutes after landing. Please state your intentions, over."

Dick replied, "Roger, flight control, we will use the autopilot. Will call you back later, over and out."

*Note: This conversation over the intercom between Dick and me was not as seamless as described here because of the interruptions necessary for normal progression of our flight toward Atlanta. There was an altitude change, several course corrections and the normal radio communications with different sectors of air traffic control. These actual flight duties mixed with the fake conversation about our landing crisis only served to make the deception more realistic.*

"Judy, you have a responsibility to your passengers and to your fellow workers. You must not in any way let on that anything other than a normal flight is in progress. All of our flight attendants are new, and I don't have time to deal with their concerns. I am only informing you of our situation because you are the A line, and it is necessary for somebody in the cabin to know."

She left the cockpit and, for a few minutes, we were concerned that maybe we had taken our hoax too far. Our worry subsided when Jake reported everything appeared as reasonably calm as their inexperience would allow.

About 20 minutes before starting our descent for Atlanta, Diane, another young flight attendant, entered the cockpit. Apparently, she had caught up with her work enough to make a quick visit to see an actual working cockpit. Dick and I were in our seats. I no longer had the oxygen mask on and had just, accidentally, dropped my pencil on the floor next to the flight yoke.

Diane spoke to Dick while I was still looking down and groping for my pencil. "Hi, I'm Diane from the coach section," she said. "Thought I'd drop in and see what it looks like up here."

I retrieved my pencil. As I raised my head and turned to greet her, one lens in my sunglasses fell out. I looked straight at her with one lens in and one lens out. She laughed, pointing at my glasses, and said, "Your . . . your glasses . . . one of them is missing."

I didn't say anything, but instead started to shake all over. I positioned my head so she could see my eye roll in its socket.

"He is very sensitive," Dick said. "Please don't make fun of his condition. It really sets him off."

"Gosh, I'm sorry . . . I thought . . . what's wrong?"

"No, no, don't say anything is wrong. That makes it worse. Now you have really set him off."

I shook with more enthusiasm. I had one hand on the flight yoke, and as I jiggled it, a minor overriding of the autopilot caused the nimble 880 Convair to vibrate slightly.

Dick said, "I'll have to calm him down. It's best that you leave."

Diane rushed out of the cockpit and back to the coach section. We did not see our flight attendants again before landing or during our long taxi to the Atlanta terminal. We thought once they had a chance to think it over and compare notes, the girls would figure out the jokes. What we didn't figure, however, was that Judy would heed Dick's instructions and tell no one about the landing pilot situation. As we turned off the runway from our landing rollout, instead of starting her after-landing duties, Judy stayed in her seat and kept looking at her watch. Suddenly, she starting waving her arms and shouting at the other flight attendants, "We're going into the take-off mode – SIT DOWN! WE'RE GOING INTO TAKE-OFF MODE!"

Two of the flight attendants looked at Judy as if she had lost her mind. But Diane looked at her with fear. When we didn't go into take-off mode, however, Judy began to see the light. By the time the airplane reached the gate, she was back in action serving the passengers. But for Diane, this was the final straw on the One-Flew-Over-the-Cuckoo's-Nest flight.

When we arrived at the gate, a confused Judy appeared at the cockpit door. "I don't know what's going on, but Diane says that as soon as the cabin door opens, she is leaving and never flying again. What have y'all done to her?"

"Judy, you must stop Diane," Captain Caravella said. "Tell her it was a joke and that I need to talk to her as soon as we secure the airplane."

But when the cabin door opened, Diane exited onto the jet-way without looking back. Dick moved quickly to catch up with her. As soon as I finished the shutdown checklist, I ran to join them. Dick grabbed my shoulder. "Steve, show her your eyes. See Diane, he's not crazy, his eyes aren't rolling – he's not shaking."

It took some doing to convince Diane we weren't lunatics, but eventually we did, and she returned to the flight and a long career as an attendant.

# PART 2

THE CITADEL

# ══ CHAPTER 2 ══
## THE SHACKLED LEG

*The difference between involvement and
commitment is like an eggs-and-ham breakfast:
the chicken was involved – the pig was committed.*

—UNKNOWN

1956: THE CITADEL — Jack Farris was terrifying. He was not just the most terrifying cadet in the Class of '58 – he was the most terrifying person any L Company freshmen had ever known.

Farris was on the gallery when we first got up. He was there before every formation. He was on the quadrangle when we rolled out. Wherever we were, he was there, yelling, correcting and intimidating. His shirt tuck was so tight you could not see a wrinkle. His brass was spotless. His shoes were like mirrors. He was perfect, and this, too, scared us. Everything that Jack Farris was, we were not, and that was bad.

We spent extra time shining and re-shining our brass and shoes. We had to report to his room for extra inspections. We had to learn the names of all the top military commanders for all service branches. We had practice sessions for shirt tucks. We would fall out of formation and then fall back into formation several times until he thought it was right. And always, we were haunted by the dreaded voice: "Halt, smack (or dumbhead, screw, do-willy, knob or any one of the other endearing names for freshmen), suck in that gut, pull your shoulders back, screw in that chin. Tell me, who is General Curtis LeMay?!"

The first three months of The Citadel plebe system were the worst, but we were only halfway through our second month. By now, we were so conditioned to fear ranking upperclassman, so convinced of their omnipotence, that we all harbored an ever-present sense of doom. Something bad could happen at any time, something we had not yet seen, and Jack Farris was the living, breathing personification of our sense of dread. We had learned a junior corporal bucking for high rank his senior year was to be avoided, but Jack Farris was bucking for regimental commander, and he was everywhere. Ray Bowley, Wayne Price and I were unlucky enough to be both in his squad and at his mess table for meals. Our mutual disdain for Farris was the passion that brought us together.

One Friday night, while preparing for SMI (Saturday Morning Inspection) and fantasizing about rotten things we could do to him, an idea was born: chain him and his roommate to their beds. We laughed and talked about the plot, and, even though our notion seemed farfetched and getting caught potentially disastrous, our bravado swept us along.

The next day after inspection we went to M. Dumas & Sons in downtown Charleston, which, in those days, was more than a clothing store. We asked about handcuffs, and, to our delight, a pair of heavy-duty shackles was produced. Thus, M. Dumas & Sons was true to its advertisement in our 1960 yearbook: "Catering to the Future Generals and Leaders of our Country."

Finding these shackles was the singular development that turned our idea from a fantasy to an actual plan. Only confiding in other freshman, we worked on the details to perfect our plan. We would gather at 3 a.m., pull nylon stockings over our heads and proceed, single file, to Jack Farris's room. The first man in line would hold open the screen door until the rest of us entered, did the deed and exited the room. He would then assist the second man in the lock-in procedure.

The secret to the lock-in was that each room had a screen door that opened out and a heavy wooden door that opened into the room. If the doors were tied together, the inside door was impossible to open. We had rehearsed this technique using the white webbing issued to make waist belts and cross-chest decorations for the full-dress uniforms. By fashioning a large knot and a loop out of the webbing, we could secure it to the wooden door handle by passing the knot through the loop. When it was time to do the lock in, the outside screen door could be shut on the webbing leaving the large knot outside, locking the doors together.

I would be third in line and the first man to enter the room. I was to leap on Jack Farris in the top bunk and immobilize him until the work was completed. The next man was Paul Passaro. His task was to contain Farris's roommate, Joe Mastroserio, who would be in the bottom bunk sleeping with his head toward Farris's feet. Man number five was Wayne Price. He was to hold Farris's leg for the shackle. Following Price was Ray Bowley, who was to hold Mastroserio's arm for the shackle. The last man was Bill Aydlotte, who was to secure the shackle to the held arm of Mastroserio and the held leg of Farris. The shackle chain was to go on the inside of the horizontal metal bed frame so that Farris and Mastroserio not only would be shackled to each other but also to the bed.

As a top-ranked junior, Farris did occasionally harass knobs from other companies, but his chief concentration was on L Company freshmen, which only strengthened our pact. We agreed that once we opened the door to start our attack, there would be no turning back. Either we would succeed or we would go down fighting. The stakes were high and only five from L Company were willing to take the risk, but the plot required seven. My own roommate declined, calling me a fool. This meant we had to go outside to M Company to recruit two knobs. The two who agreed professed to hate Farris, but not with the passion of the core group. As such, they were assigned the less demanding jobs of holding the doors and arranging the webbing for the lock-in.

An operation of this order required intense attention to detail. We examined the shackles closely, assessing their size, durability and configuration. In testing them on legs of varying sizes, we determined they might be too small for our intended victims. The shackles fit Bill Aydlotte's legs, so all we needed to do was compare his legs to those of Farris and Mastroserio.

At a scheduled yearly physical test (PT), we got our chance. Upperclassmen and plebes were on the field together either doing a part of the test or resting. Aydlotte got within a couple of feet of Mastroserio and then Farris, while we nonchalantly passed by, sizing up their legs. Based on this, we were confident the shackles would fit.

There had been much discussion about what would happen if any of us were captured. It went without saying that we would not cave under questioning and name anyone. But we did wonder how much pressure we would take before agreeing to open the shackles, which we figured out, could be picked with the end of a disassembled metal shoe horn. So the day before D-Night, we filled the locks on the shackles with glue and threw the key into the marsh behind the tailor shop.

My alarm went off at 2:45 a.m. My roommate grunted, wished me luck and went back to sleep. Dressed in pants and t-shirt, I picked up the nylon stocking I would use to disguise my face and proceeded to the gallery. The plan seemed genius in a gathering of comrades talking about brave deeds planned for a future date. But, out of uniform, alone on the gallery at 3 a.m., I wondered if my roomie might be right in calling me a fool. The place was cold and quiet – deathly quiet – except for the doleful clanging of the empty flag attachment against its flagpole. Adrenaline shot through my system when I saw several figures approaching. I did not move.

"Hey, Taylor," one of them whispered. I breathed a sigh of relief. Soon the attack team was assembled. Shivering from the cold and fear, we pulled the stockings over our heads and fell into line according to the order of tasks.

We knew the doors would open, because, under the code of the honor system, it was against regulation to lock them. Like the well-oiled machine we were, we set our precision plan in motion. I began my sprint the moment the freshman from M Company clicked open the door latch, thus ensuring that I would be at full tilt when I hurled myself at Farris as he lay asleep in his bunk. But, as I charged into the room, all the lights snapped on.

It turned out Farris had rigged a Rube Goldberg-style mechanism involving a ramrod under the light switches with loops and strings so that when the door opened, it pulled the string that connected to the ramrod that snapped on the lights. Once again, Farris was perfect.

But I was already in motion and my pledge to continue, no matter what, carried me through. Farris was asleep on his back in the top bunk. I leapt on him before he could move. Grasping the metal runners on each side of his bunk, I put my shoulder in the hollow of his neck and pulled down, forcing it into his throat. He struggled for a minute and then relaxed.

From earlier observations, I knew Farris was in excellent condition. At the previously mentioned PT test there were only two perfect scores in the corps. Jack Farris made one; the other was made by the frightened plebe now on top of him. Thinking he would be difficult to contain, I overdid the squeezing and, as it turned out, choked him to unconsciousness.

Meanwhile, our two recruits from the other company, on seeing the lights, had turned and run. This left the doors unattended, eliminating any possibility of a lock-in. In the confusion, it took a few beats for the rest of the dedicated L Company knobs to enter. They ran square into Mastroserio as he was getting out of bed and a hellacious fight broke out with him. He was screaming and swearing like a wild man. I maintained my position while the others tried to get Mastroserio back in bed. He was as strong as a bull and by now was on the floor.

The commotion woke other upperclassmen, who soon arrived. When we thought all was lost, Bill Aydlotte still managed to get the shackle on Farris's leg and snap the other end to the steel horizontal bar of the bed.

The room was now full of fighting cadets and more jammed the door to get in. I rolled from the top bunk to the floor, then, on all fours, crawled through the melee and out the door to the gallery as more upperclassmen tried to get in. Somehow, no one noticed me recede into the darkness.

As I lay on my bunk listening to the bellowing and screaming one gallery below, I silently cheered for my buddies, hoping they would all escape. I would later learn that Farris regained consciousness and, not knowing he was shackled, leapt out of bed. His leg stayed behind and he ended up hanging by it, upside down, yelling for the knobs to stand at attention, his leg bruised and bleeding.

But there I was, in the quiet calm of my room, contemplating the reality of the situation. I had been a vocal proponent of the plan, had rehearsed it in my mind so many times I could play it forwards and backwards without thinking. Reality tasted a whole lot different than fantasy, however. We had not only physically attacked upperclassmen, but we had attacked the most exalted juniors in the school. There would be no way to explain that this was a mere prank. It would be viewed as insubordination of the highest order and could result in expulsion. Reality tasted even worse when I found out the other four conspirators from L Company had been caught.

Following the incident, several upperclassmen came to my room and questioned me. Eventually, all the knobs in L Company were questioned and, though each knew who the culprits were, they all gave the same answer I did: "Sir, no excuse, sir."

To say that Jack Farris was mad was an understatement. He had been injured, his authority compromised, but worst of all, he had been humiliated. More than one upperclassman found the situation amusing. The more the others snickered, the more Farris raged. He ordered the knobs to get the key and free him. Not an option, he was informed. And so the raging continued, reaching a kind of snarling crescendo when someone suggested picking the lock and discovered it was filled with glue.

Ray Bowley had the unenviable task of digging out the dried glue. During this time the anger would build, and Farris would yell at Bowley. He, properly so, would stop working on the lock and go into a brace, which slowed the process.

In the end, Farris kept all of the punishment in-company and did not bring it to the attention of any above his rank. To ascend to a higher station, talent alone was not enough. It required good judgment and instincts. If it were widely known that lowly freshmen found Farris so despicable they would ambush him in his sleep, his leadership abilities might be called into question. Instead, every night Farris required the four knobs to report to his room at 2 a.m.

in full dress uniform, ready for SMI inspection. But this nightly schedule was also hard on him. If he were to be regimental commander and someday General Farris, he needed to keep up his grades. After a couple of weeks of lost sleep, he discontinued the inspections.

Years later, I piloted a C-130 to Pope Air Force Base to do a troop drop for the 82nd Airborne Division at Fort Bragg. We were parked on the ramp while the troops mustered behind our aircraft waiting for us to clear them to load. When I went back to check the cargo compartment, I noticed someone from the army inspecting my aircraft door. As I approached to ask what he was doing, the man looked up. In that moment, everything came rushing back. I almost stood at attention. It was Jack Farris, and I still feared him.

Jack did become regimental commander of The Citadel, and he retired from the army as a three star general.

# CHAPTER 3
## THE WORST DAY

*A man who carries a cat by the tail
learns something he can learn no other way.*

—MARK TWAIN

1956 – 1958: THE CITADEL — I arrived on campus with a cocky attitude, which guaranteed I would be singled out for extra trouble.

Aspiring freshman cadets reported eight days ahead of the main corps where they would be trained, threatened and pushed to exhaustion by a select cadre, so that the unseasoned knobs would begin fitting into the system when the rest of the cadets arrived. They called it hell week. But as far as I could tell, hell week was not confined to those first eight days. The harassment and strict training persisted the rest of the semester, the only difference being that we also took classes. By the third week, I was feeling the strain. My roommate had already quit.

To this day I remember our tormenters – their names and faces are affixed in my memory like tattoos: Terrell, Willhite, Farris, Mastroserio, and then there was Conley, our company commander, so far above me that he would look at me like I was a cockroach that needed to be smashed.

My survival code was simple – make it through the next five minutes. But on this particular day, five minutes seemed more like an eternity, followed by another five minutes. At morning formation, I had been summarily chewed out, though to my knowledge I had committed no infraction beyond the space I occupied and the breath I drew. After complying with the order to stand at attention during breakfast, I barely had anything to eat. Arriving 30 seconds late to class, the professor threatened to drop me from the course. On my way to my next class, I was stopped and reprimanded because my hat was on wrong. In a panic not to be late, I ran at full-tilt down the hall and collided with another freshman. I snapped. He snapped. We both assumed the collision was deliberate.

A raging fistfight broke out while books and other classmates scattered. The fight was quickly stopped by upperclassmen, and we both received stern reprimands while standing at attention. The ranking cadet stepped forward and announced he would take the necessary corrective action. We were instructed to show up at the gym at 3 p.m. This freshman adversary was larger than I was and looked to be quite fit. But when we were told we would be fighting with boxing gloves, my confidence rose. I had done some boxing and believed this would make up for the difference in size. Of course, my opponent was thinking I was a punk, and he was going to mop the floor with me.

At three o'clock sharp we reported to the gym, donned the gloves and were told the rules: There would be only one round, and it would last until one of us gave up. There would not be the question of who got in the best blows, or who was the more aggressive at the end of a designated number of rounds. It would simply be a test of wills and endurance.

Having had time to cool off, I no longer felt anger toward the big guy, but nonetheless realized the stakes. I was determined to humble my opponent.

We started the match with his attempt to finish me quickly with a roundhouse punch, and if it had connected, I would indeed have been finished. I got in a few blows while he was off balance, but they did not do the necessary damage. I managed to get inside his longer reach and land some more. Then he connected, landing a day involved poor judgment stemming from my aforementioned attitude.

Mr. Hardy was a sophomore and, as such, did not hold rank or have responsibility for the lowly plebes. However, he was an upperclassman who was to be respected by freshmen. For some reason he took a dislike to me and chastised me more than I thought was within his authority. The whole corps had been to a school meeting at the chapel. We returned individually across the parade ground. In his obnoxious way, Hardy walked behind me offering a constant stream of ridicule.

My temper flared as I turned. "Hardy, why don't you join me for a fight, right here, and we will see how tough you are."

It's never smart to display temper, but to challenge an upperclassman to a fight is not just out of line. It's stupid.

"Mr. Taylor, you have just stepped in it. We will see you in your room."

I knew I had made a big mistake, and when he said *we*, I feared the worst.

Back in my room, I was warning my roommate of the coming trouble when our door burst open with a loud bang. In walked not Mr. Hardy, but most of the ranking cadets of our company – the ones with the power. The first sergeant was there along with most of the junior corporals bucking for rank. They may not have thought much of Hardy picking on the knobs, but insubordination would not be tolerated.

One of the cadets picked up an M-1 rifle from its rack and threw it at me. As I caught it, I was told to get on the wall. I was familiar with the command. It required placing your heels as high as possible up on the wall while your toes remained on the floor. The rifle was held across the chest with the muzzle pointing off the left shoulder at port arms while the stomach, shoulders and chin were as far back and in as possible.

The rapid fire screaming and snarling came from so many directions I had difficulty understanding what was said. There were corporals on each side and one in front of me barking at me with such ferocity I could feel their spit hitting my face and dripping down my neck.

Finally, the company first sergeant stepped forward and the room fell silent. "You have committed gross insubordination – it will not be tolerated. You are through. You will be leaving The Citadel one way or the other. To save yourself some trouble, you can resign now, or we will force you out, but you are leaving."

Man, this was bad – what had I done? I knew I would be in trouble as soon as I had let my temper take control – but this – the whole school seemed to be in agreement that I should be destroyed.

We were taught that there are only three things a freshman can say to avoid trouble: Yes, sir – no, sir – no excuse, sir. When I was pressed for an answer I responded, "No excuse, sir!"

"Dumbhead, I did not ask you for an excuse. I asked you for an answer."

"No excuse, sir!"

The first sergeant stepped back. A brief conference took place, and from out of this caldron of wrath stepped a junior private by the name of J.O. Duberly. I had heard rumors that he had belonged to a street gang in Savannah. I also had heard that he was in some kind of trouble and was leaving The Citadel.

"Mr. Taylor, I am leaving – nothing more can be done to me. If you are so tough, come off that wall and let's see."

They were determined to run me out of the school – I was scared, real scared. Not of physical harm, but of not making it at The Citadel. I could see a no-win situation developing here. I could come off the wall, fight Duberly, and whether I won or lost, I would be officially charged.

"What do you say, Mr. Taylor?"

"No excuse, sir."

"You're yellow – all mouth and no fight. Are you going to fight or not?"

"No excuse, sir."

Though by now my feet and ankles ached, I stayed up on the wall. The rifle I was holding at port arms was starting to sag. I relaxed my chin slightly because I felt a little dizzy. This prompted the corporals to step forward and begin a new round of screaming.

For more than an hour, the group hurled more threats and insults at me. Eventually, though, they had enough and walked away. But even this was not my worst day.

A week later I was ordered to report to the room of two juniors. They were not top ranking and had not been to my room on that night, but they took it on themselves to get in on my harassment. Every Citadel class has heard about how much tougher things were during the old days. One of the rumors was about the green stool treatment. In every cadet's room was a sturdy wooden box used to store the equipment for shining shoes. In the old days this box was painted green, although in my day it was brown. The freshman supposedly was ordered to squat on this box while a broom handle was placed behind his knees. Usually he was threatened with some dire punishment if he fell off the box, however, the broom handle cut off circulation to his legs so that he would eventually fall off.

I was ordered to get on the green stool (although it was brown). To their amazement, I refused. After much verbal abuse, I reminded them that it fell under the anti-hazing rules, and if they pushed me further I would go to the school commandant. This was humiliating to them and there was not a pleasant way to save face. My extra harassment, albeit legal, continued unabated for many weeks, but in time it gradually subsided. My worst day was still to come.

TWO YEARS LATER — The Citadel suited me. I had learned a lot and was doing well as a cadet of the junior class. I had made corporal, which was the only rank to be held by a junior. I had been a member of the training cadre for the new freshmen, and had the responsibility of being the head of a dining table in the mess hall. I had passed all but the final elimination to make the prestigious Summerall Guards. I was in love with a wonderful girl, was well on my way to graduating with a degree in civil engineering and had a contract to attend Air Force flight school.

Trouble came unexpectedly from an unexpected situation. In the middle of dinner a freshman walked up to my table, where I was the head cadet, and shot me the bird. This was blatant insubordination, and I had learned the hard way that it will not be tolerated. Leaping from my chair, I chased the knob back to his seat. As I started to write down his name, the head of his mess table, a senior, ordered me to stop. This was now a dilemma. If I reported the freshman, I would be out of line for disobeying the senior's order and in violation of the long-standing tradition of the class system, but this could not go unpunished. By now, much of the mess hall, especially the freshmen, were watching to see what would happen. My indignation overrode my sense of self-preservation, and I declared in a loud voice, "Dumbhead, you will be charged with insubordination and suffer the full extent of the punishment it brings."

Hard times were to follow.

The next day I received demerits for 20 trumped-up infractions, all reported by seniors. These reports continued all week.

On that Friday, the day Summerall Guards were to be announced, I woke up tired and achy. I knew I was coming down with a cold. I dragged myself out of bed and headed to class only to find that I had flunked a major test in mechanics.

At noon on Fridays, it was customary for the names of cadets who had strayed from the straight and narrow to have their names and punishments read aloud over the intercom. While the corps stood in the noon formation, cadets learned their fate as it was broadcast for all to hear.

The previous weekend several of us had been stopped for returning to campus in civilian clothes, but because of the circumstances, we did not expect to be punished. Hearing my name over the loudspeaker was bad enough, but I was shocked to learn I was not only restricted, had tours to walk, but was also reduced to the rank of private. This would cost me my position at the head of the table and hurt my chances for rank in my senior year. It also removed me from the cadet cadre.

After lunch, I proceeded to the post office to check my mail. I had not seen my girlfriend for several months, but perhaps a letter from her would cheer me. The letter was there, but the bad news continued. Time and distance were too much; she thought it wise, for now, to go our separate ways. With the obligatory, "I will always care for you, Steve, and never forget you," I was shafted when it hurt the most.

I didn't have time to worry about the day's developments anymore. It was time to report for the final tryout for the Summerall Guards. I had done well up to then, and I was optimistic I would make the final cut.

The seniors on the old guard directed the tryouts. After the last cuts were made, we were told to take a seat in the stadium where we had been working. The head of the previous year's guard stepped forward and announced that those of us seated were the Bond Volunteers and next year's Summerall Guards. Just as he said this, another senior cadet stopped him and whispered something. They both looked at me and whispered some more. A third senior joined them and there was more discussion. The head guard pointed at me and ordered, "Taylor, stand up." When I stood he said, "You are cut." More payback for violating the class system.

Sitting in my room that night, I lowered my forehead onto my desk and reflected on the day. My cold was worse; I had flunked a major mechanics test, lost my rank, was sentenced to walk tours and serve restrictions, would lose my mess and the position on the cadre, lost my girlfriend and had unfairly been cut from the Summerall Guards. The seniors were piling on the demerits, which would bring more trouble with the commandant's department. This could cost me my pilot contract. This was a disaster – THIS WAS THE WORST DAY OF MY LIFE!

A friend, who was somewhat of a cynic, once said when asked what was so great about The Citadel: "If you wreck your car, your wife leaves you, and you get fired from your job all in the same day, you will be prepared because you can remember a worse day at The Citadel."

He was only partly joking.

Governor Hollings arrived on campus to speak while I was starting my punishment. The Citadel was a South Carolina state school and Governor Hollings, a graduate of The Citadel, used his power as head of state to grant amnesty to wayward cadets. This included my own transgressions, releasing me from my tours and restrictions. The following spring semester my rank was restored. The Summerall Guards ended up being short one man, and as soon as my classmates took over, they remembered my unjust treatment and I was reinstated. I passed mechanics and graduated with a civil engineering degree. I entered Air Force pilot training the following spring. And with time – lots of time – the pain of my lost love faded.

The greatest way to build self-esteem is to overcome adversity. We love what gives self-esteem. The Citadel was an exercise in overcoming adversity – the word love and The Citadel don't seem compatible – but I do love what it did for me.

# PART 3

AIR FORCE

# ≡ CHAPTER 4 ≡
## HELL BENT

*The idea was to prove at every foot of the way up that you were one of the elected and anointed ones who had the right stuff and could move higher and higher and even – ultimately, God willing, one day that you might be able to join that special few at the very top, that elite who had the capacity to bring tears to men's eyes, the very Brotherhood of the Right Stuff itself.*

—TOM WOLFE (THE RIGHT STUFF)

*Me climbing into the T-37.*

1961: LAREDO, TEXAS — Just west of Mobile I passed an Austin Healy with the top down. A young man about my age eyed me with disapproval as I sped by. In another ten miles, he passed me. The next time we were close he made an airplane flying motion with his hand, and I knew he was also on his way to Laredo, Texas, for flight training. We ate together, refueled together and became friends by the time the sweet smell of desert spring flooded across our open tops. Mark Hinckley and I shared the same dream. After the physicals, testing and years of preparation to be accepted we were going to be Air Force jet pilots. We were both licensed private pilots and graduate engineers. Our optimism and energy were boundless, but little did we know of the agony that lay ahead – of the 60 inflated male egos that reported that first day, 30 would wash out. Mark Hinckley would be one of them.

Air Force pilot training was a high-intensity pressure cooker. By the time a student withstood the selection process, the rigorous academics, the concentrated training schedule and the fear of dying, he considered himself a cut above every other human being on earth. This attitude was encouraged, because to believe you can master the tasks that appear impossible, a new pilot must feel capable of mastering what no ordinary mortal would attempt.

I had staked my identity and reputation on becoming a jet pilot, spreading the word to all who knew me. Failure was not an option. But I also knew the odds and I knew the prize. I had heard that every flight school graduate represented one out of a hundred who had tried to go for the silver wings. I had tackled the studies and training with vigor. I could explain the airplane operating systems in detail. I could recite procedures for any emergency in my sleep. But after four weeks of training, I sat in my 1957 Thunderbird, a jet pilot's car, about to be washed out of the program before I ever took my first jet solo.

My instructor had hated me from the very first lesson when I had barfed all over the airplane. He went by the call sign of Grossvater – not Ace, not Viper, not Badger, but Grossvater. He had been stationed in Germany and thought it was cool. I thought it was dumb. He was a screamer and through his profanity and ridicule, I gleaned that jet pilots don't get sick and therefore I would never be one. In our entire time together, he never complimented a thing I did. I was stupid, I was uncoordinated, I didn't pay attention, I should save the time for him, me and the government and just quit the program. I could take the insults and the screaming – after all I had graduated from The Citadel. But there was one thing that torqued my jaws: he called me a *pussy* – me, the boxer, number one on the physical training test, the Citadel cadet that had tweaked the system and taken everything they could throw. But this was Grossvater's description of any pilot who got sick. And boy did I get sick. I became an aficionado of the barf bag. I barfed on final approach, I barfed on rolling out of the pitch, I even barfed in the top of a loop (because that's where the G's were reduced enough to allow it to come up). I learned to fly with one hand on the stick and a barf bag in my throttle hand.

I began to acclimate as the training sessions progressed, but when I had not yet gotten sick, Grossvater would take the airplane, as if he were going to show me a maneuver, and ring it out until he made me sick. This is when it began to dawn on me that he was determined to wash me out.

Some motion sickness was accepted on the first few flights, but there were limits. Grossvater was pleased that I had barfed the limit, and now I was facing an interview with the flight surgeon. I knew what this meant. The flight surgeon would cite "incompatible physical conditions" and begin the paperwork to eliminate me from the flying program.

So here I was, dreading to start the car, all dressed up in jet pilot clothes, a pilot wannabe, a *pussy,* who suffered from motion sickness. Truth be told, I had gotten sick at rides at the county fair, at sea, in a J-3 Piper Cub, and even on a swing.

I'm not sure what was worse – the thought of my own lifetime dream spoiled, or the heartache of telling my parents. I knew they were proud of me and had bragged about their son the jet pilot. While wrestling with these thoughts, tormented by the prospect of failure, I remembered something my father did back when I was eleven years old. He was desperate to hold on to our farm, but, as hard as he worked, he had been unable to make enough money from farming alone. We had an old empty tenant house that he rented for a small sum on a temporary basis to the power company. Construction crews used it to store their equipment during the construction of a new high-tension power line. Late in the afternoon, crews would gather outside this tenant house while they put away their tools and supplies.

One day the line supervisor stopped by and my father struck up a conversation with him, inquiring if the power company was hiring.

"Not unless you are a bulldozer operator. We lost ours today and we need one immediately or everything comes to a halt," the man said.

Dad paused before speaking. Then he asked the man what kind of dozer they had and was told it was a Caterpillar D8. The supervisor commented that it was going to be hard to find another operator on such short notice.

I had never known my father to tell a lie. I also knew he'd never been on a bulldozer in his life, let alone operated one. So when I heard what came out of his mouth next, I was stunned.

"Sir, this stop you made here today was a fortunate thing. Before I started farming, I was an experienced D8 operator. Since the farming business has not gone well this year, I could use the work."

"Be there Monday morning at eight o'clock, and we'll see if you are going to work out."

My father did not miss a beat. "These D8s are wonderful machines, but sometimes they are a little temperamental and each one has its own quirks. If I could talk to the previous operator, I can address any of these mechanical issues and have it running smoothly when you arrive Monday morning."

The man gave him the name and phone number of the previous driver, who was taking leave to undergo treatment for cancer. Dad called him and after a lengthy conversation about the new power line, the man's illness and the dozer, the man agreed to come out on Sunday and go over the D8 with him. My dad practiced operating the rig until dark. By Monday morning, he was a convincing dozer operator.

So on the day I was ordered to see the Air Force flight surgeon,

I dropped by my BOQ room and pondered the seriousness of what I was about to do. I did not go to see the surgeon. Instead, after about an hour in my room, I returned to the flight shack and announced that the flight surgeon had diagnosed my continued motioned sickness as a slow working stomach virus that would subside in a few days.

Two days later, I strapped in next to an irritated Grossvater. During my fake flight surgeon visit, I had also decided if this was going to work I had to change instructors. This was touchy business as we had been warned not to try it.

Our flight was normal, that is, he screamed, and close to the end, after he jerked the airplane through some violent maneuvers, I barfed. But then something strange happened: he shut up and let me work my way back to the field in peace. For a brief moment I thought, maybe this will work. Then, as I rolled out on final approach, he said, "You dumb shit."

That was all it took. I let go of the stick and looked at him. "You have the airplane. I will never fly for you again."

"Taylor, I'm not flying, you're flying. Take over and land or you will kill us both."

"Then we die, but I will never fly with you in an airplane again."

He took over just in time to land, mumbling something about me being through with flight school forever.

I went straight to the squadron commander's office. I started telling my story and he cut me short. "You can have a new instructor."

My new instructor was a godsend. On our first flight, he told me we would practice some aerobatics, and if I started to feel woozy we could do something else until it passed. Soon, airsickness was over forever and my confidence swelled.

With my first solo under my belt and my cookies reliably in place, it was time to prepare for a solo flight out of the airport area. We were told not to fly faster than 350 knots, but I knew the airplane would do 400 knots. Leveling at 16,000 feet, I pushed the throttle to the red line, feeling an adrenaline rush as the airspeed indicator hit the barber pole at 400 knots. At that moment, nothing else mattered, just the open sky, that machine made for speed and me. I lost track of time.

Reality only struck when I suddenly realized my allotted time was almost over. Now racing against the clock, I turned the plane to head back to the base, never easing up on the throttle or altitude, hell bent on getting there within the allotted time. Approaching the airport, I popped the speed brake to slow down and help my descent. As I did, I could feel the entire machine vibrate with the strain of the sudden extension of the metal surface into the slipstream. It took longer than I expected to adjust the speed and altitude to traffic pattern requirements and though I managed to get it there, something was wrong. Too much vibration – too much power. Desperately searching for the cause, I turned and looked through the back of the cockpit bubble at the tail section. And then I saw it. My God! The tail was bent!

It took me a moment to process what I was seeing. I looked again. No question, one section of the horizontal stabilizer was distorted. My mind raced. What had I done to cause this to happen? And what did it mean? I thought about ejecting but quickly rejected the idea. I thought about calling the tower and discussing my situation with an instructor, but I hesitated. I knew he would ask me what I had been doing with the airplane, and I would have to admit to speeding.

I exited the traffic pattern to think, going over the flight in my mind. The speed brake! It was still extended. I quickly retracted it and the vibration stopped. Problem solved! But when I looked back at the tail, it was still bent. Would I be able to land with this much damage? There was so much I didn't know. My heart raced. I could hear my loud rapid breathing through my headset. I was already late – *come on Taylor, either land or bail out.* I braced for the worst. Impossibly, miraculously, the plane felt normal as I touched down and came to a stop.

I climbed out of the cockpit, desperate to see the damage to the tail. My mind reeled. But when I looked, the tail was as sleek and straight as it had been when I climbed aboard. I was baffled. I climbed back into the cockpit, closed the canopy, and, as I did, noticed the mechanic looking at me as he waited to service the plane. Doubtless he wondered about the stupid student practicing getting out and back in the plane. But I had a mystery to solve. A moment later, I solved it. Damn, was I the only one who didn't know this, or was I the only one who had looked directly behind me? The distortion to the tail came from the rear convex cockpit glass.

With fits and starts, I was working my way through the many phases of flight training. By the time I was on my first night solo, my confidence was high, and I was relaxed at 21,000 feet, looking down on an occasional toy car, a few lights here and there. Except for the whine of my engines it was quiet. The red glow of the cockpit, the faint outline of the distant horizon under the starlight – then I understood the poet, John Magee: "Oh! I have slipped the surly bonds of earth . . . and, while with silent lifting mind I've trod . . . put out my hand, and touched the face of God."

With six months of training in the T-37 jet, I had successfully completed basic, cross country navigation, aerobatics and formation flying. It was time to report for my final instrument check. This would be my last check before graduating from the T-37 to the larger T-33 jet trainer. The T-33 was the trainer version of the first Air Force jet fighter, the F-80 Shooting Star. I was so close to becoming a real jet jock I could taste it. But I wasn't there yet.

*T-33s in formation – the real jets.*

After a short briefing, I walked to the flight line with the instructor who was designated as my flight examiner for the final instrument check. I did the walk-around inspection and strapped in, rapidly going through the now familiar preflight procedures. We all wore the standard flight helmet with oxygen mask and hose. Because the T-37 was unpressurized, it was necessary to breathe with an oxygen mask at higher altitudes. We used an acronym to remember all the steps for the oxygen check – PD M<sup>C</sup>CRIPE: pressure, diaphragm, mask, connection – CONNECTION. I was momentarily distracted as my instructor repeated the altimeter setting he had just heard over the radio. Unaware that I had skipped the most important step of actually connecting the oxygen hose to the regulator, completion of the other items on the oxygen checklist were for naught.

After we took the runway, the examiner reached into his bag and took out the blinders used for instrument flying. These fit onto my helmet so I could see only the instruments directly in front of my eyes. That effectively killed any chance of looking outside the jet to determine the situation.

We climbed to 21,000 feet and went through various instrument maneuvers. Hypoxia onset at this altitude is an insidious condition. I had been through the altitude chamber and watched my fellow pilots go through very rapid hypoxia at 35,000 feet and had done so myself. At that altitude, the time of useful consciousness is about 15 seconds without oxygen. But at 21,000 feet the onset happens slowly. Not only is there no discomfort, gradual deprivation of oxygen results in euphoria.

At first I was alert and doing well. But after about 20 minutes, I started to get sloppy. Finally, my instructor looked at me and said, "Taylor, what's the matter with you? You're off your altitude. You're off your heading and you're all over the sky."

I looked over at him, and though he couldn't see it through my mask, I was grinning. "Uh – I'll get it – just a minute." I actually thought I was doing great.

"Taylor, something's wrong with you. Check your oxygen."

I slowly looked at my oxygen regulator. The regulator should have blinked every time I took a breath, but I was too far gone to see anything wrong. I turned and gave him a blank look.

"Check your hose connection," he shouted, "NOW!"

I found the loose hose connection, but by now I was so daffy, instead of hooking it to the regulator, I tried to stick the end of the hose in my mouth, but it kept hitting the mask.

At that point I passed out. My next memory was coming to and going into convulsions. Even though conscious, I could not control the shaking and jerking of my body and, for a short while, I couldn't talk. Though scary, this is a temporary part of the recovery process. But under the stress of the situation, my poor instructor forgot that detail and thought I was dying. We were in a steep dive toward the airport, and I heard the call to the tower.

"Mayday – mayday – mayday, I have an incapacitated student. I need an ambulance. I say again, I have an incapacitated student. I need an ambulance."

By the time we were on approach, I had recovered and tried to convince the flight examiner that I was all right, but he obviously had doubts. I could see an ambulance and fire truck off to one side of the runway. As we taxied onto the apron, three medics ran from the ambulance with a stretcher. I tried again to convince my instructor I was fine.

"This is precautionary," the instructor said. "Just do what they say. I will shut down the left engine and leave the right one running. Keep your helmet on so the noise doesn't damage your ears."

The medics, of course, had no idea what condition I was in, so they tried to grab me and put me on the stretcher. I resisted and walked to the ambulance with a medic on either side holding my arms. I was allowed to sit in the ambulance with one medic next me and one across from me still convinced in my mind that I was okay. But as each medic asked me a question, I found myself having to turn my head and look straight at him in order to see him. I suddenly realized I had no peripheral vision whatsoever. And then it hit me. Oxygen starvation could cause vision impairment. I saw my life flash in front of me, realizing it would mean the end of my flying career. In a panic, I shouted, "I've got gun barrel vision! I can't see! I've got gun barrel vision!"

One of the medics calmly reached up and removed my instrument blinders and said, "Lieutenant, does this help?"

"Uh . . . yes," I sheepishly replied.

# ═ CHAPTER 5 ═
## TRAINING FOR CHAOS

*"The reason the American Army does so well
in wartime is that war is chaos, and the American Army
practices it on a daily basis."*

—A POST-WAR DEBRIEFING FROM A GERMAN GENERAL

1962-1964: ALL OVER THE WORLD — It has been said that no battle plan survives the first enemy engagement and that war is the most complex of human endeavors. Trying to duplicate the complexity and terror of war with military training is like having a bullfight with a goat.

## SLICK DZ

I was a lowly co-pilot assigned to a tactical squadron at Sewart Air Force Base. Gen. Walter C. Sweeney was the four star hard-charging new commander of the Tactical Air Command (TAC). He had been a general in the Strategic Air Command (SAC) under the tutelage of the bigger than life, cigar-chomping Gen. Curtis LeMay. In those days SAC had the responsibility for our nation's nuclear deterrence and the mutually assured destruction principle. It was a responsibility of epic proportions, allowing no room for mistakes. Some thought Gen. Sweeney did not possess the necessary flexibility to run the Tactical Air Command with its many assorted missions. He had a reputation for being mean and unforgiving, especially to colonels in command, and was infamous for firing them on the spot with no regard for the consequences of his actions on a career commander.

Operation Swift Strike, carried out in the Carolinas, was the largest war game ever mounted by TAC. Undertaken in conjunction with the army, our wing headquarters was set up temporarily at Pope Air Force Base at Ft. Bragg, N.C. The wing commander was Col. Parker, an ambitious, high-strung bird colonel, nervous and well aware of his peril under the command of Gen. Sweeney.

Our C-130 crew was ordered to fly to Pope from our home base at Sewart, but when we got there, no one knew why we were sent. We checked into the BOQ, and each day we reported to the headquarters building to discover that everyone was too busy to figure out why we were there. After sitting around for several hours, we would return to the BOQ. This schedule provided us with ample time to play at the officers' club, so we didn't complain.

On one of our sit-arounds at wing operations, we observed a Gen. Sweeney moment. There was a call from the general's headquarters with an order to have 20 airplanes over Slick Drop Zone (Slick DZ) in 15 minutes. Col. Parker's office took the call, setting into motion some high-test discord.

It didn't take much to ascertain this was an impossible order. Some of the airplanes were on the ground, and the crews were either at the mess hall or the officers' club. Some were flying on other missions. It would exceed the General's allotted time just locating the necessary airplanes and crews. Once the crews got to the airplanes, it would take more time for startup, taxi and takeoff, and Slick DZ, though close by, still required a few minutes of flying time.

Col. Parker came out of his office red-faced and agitated. He yelled for the lieutenant who was assigned to him as a gofer. "Go to the officers' club and the mess hall, find the crews and send them to their airplanes. Tell them to prepare for takeoff immediately. They will get their instructions over the radio."

The young officer left at a dead run, but quickly returned. Before he could speak, he met a verbal barrage from Col. Parker. "What the hell are you doing back here?! I told you to find the crews!"

"But sir, the van is not there. I think a crew took it to the mess hall."

"Dammit, I don't have time to babysit you. Figure it out, but get those crew members to their airplanes – now do it!"

The lieutenant ran for the exit once again, and this time he did not return.

As this scene was taking place, the hot line in the Colonel's office started ringing – IT WAS GEN. SWEENEY.

"Colonel, I want you to join me for a viewing of your operation at Slick DZ immediately."

Col. Parker could see his career going down the tubes. One thing he knew for sure, it was absolutely necessary that he join Gen. Sweeney as soon as possible to defend his performance. Maybe he could explain to the general why his airplanes were late.

He grabbed his hat and ran for the door, but like the young lieutenant, soon returned.

"MY STAFF CAR IS GONE! MY STAFF CAR IS GONE! MY STAFF CAR IS GONE!"

His voice was at a strange high pitch, as if he were trying out for an operatic solo.

The young lieutenant had taken Parker at his word to figure it out. Since the base was secure and no one but Col. Parker was allowed to use his staff car, he always left the keys in the ignition. The lieutenant saw the keys and off he went to find the crews. By now Col. Parker was jumping up and down and yelling incoherently. There was no transportation available for his rendezvous with Gen. Sweeney and nothing he could do about it but rant.

## TENSE ON TENTS

A year after Swift Strike, TAC initiated operation Desert Strike. I participated in this war game also, and enjoyed it for the most part. It took place in the desert area of southern California and Arizona. We were quartered in temporary Quonset huts and provided with a small desert traversing vehicle called an Army Mule. When we weren't flying, we explored the arid land, chasing jackrabbits and picking up petrified wood.

Our mission was to haul whatever some higher authority determined needed relocating. The most memorable trip was a flight to a remote dirt strip about 50 miles northwest of Yuma. We had the cargo compartment loaded to the roof with tents.

After the giant cloud of dust cleared following our landing, an army major approached the airplane. We lowered the cockpit stairs and he eagerly inquired, "What did you bring us?"

When we told him tents, I thought he would cry, but he quickly got the impulse under control and yelled instead. "Tents! More goddamn tents?! Do you see that giant storage shelter over there? It is full of tents. We already have over 10,000 and you bring more. We have no food, water is running low, fuel is running low, and we don't even have a stove or a shovel. We pee in the desert with the Gila monsters and rattlesnakes. We are freezing at night, and you sons-of-bitches bring more goddamn tents?!"

We felt sorry for the major and upon returning to our point of departure reported his predicament to the operations officer. His response: "Damn, a plane just departed for that outpost."

I had to inquire, "Do you know what it was transporting?"

"Tents," he said. "Two thousand tents."

## GREEN LIGHT

When not playing war games, we still trained most of the time. I went to jump school and did temporary duty in Panama, Saudi Arabia, Iran and France, flying all over the world primarily for training. While flying in Europe, our crew was chosen as lead aircraft to demonstrate the latest evolution in troop carrier formation called Close Look. It was developed back in the States and the purpose of the exercise was to convince the brass to accept the new technique in Europe. Bleachers had been erected right next to the drop zone, so close the generals and VIPs would be able to walk out and shake hands with the landing paratroops.

In a Close Look formation, the airplanes fly at 200 feet above the ground, strung out five seconds apart at 300 knots airspeed. Just prior to the drop zone, each in turn would zoom up to drop altitude. This zoom dissipated speed rapidly to 130 knots. When the troops were all out, each plane dove down to regain its speed. The procedure was designed for minimum exposure time to ground fire while flying slowly at drop altitude.

The weather did not cooperate. We were in and out of broken clouds with marginal visibility. Our squadron commander, Lt. Col. Livers, was riding with us along with an extra navigator. My job was to turn on the green light signaling the troops to exit. My aircraft commander (A/C) suggested we might consider aborting the mission but Livers wanted to press on. This was his show and, by God, it had to work.

It is very difficult to identify points on the ground while flying fast and low, but with poor visibility it was nearly impossible even with two highly experienced navigators. They were uneasy, constantly jabbering, checking instruments, and looking out the window for something they could recognize.

Navigator #1: "Is that the popup point?"

Navigator #2: "I don't see it, uh . . . maybe, yeah . . . ."

Navigator #1: "Popup, popup."

The aircraft commander wiped off the power and pulled up to drop altitude. Shortly after, I heard, "Green light." I flipped the switch, and 65 paratroopers jumped into the clouds.

The flight crew behind us had no idea where they were, but they knew we had lots of experience on our airplane – so we must be right. They saw us in and out of the clouds and dropped their troops based on our drop, and so it went for the other airplanes, each dropping on the ship in front.

The VIP's and generals could hear the distant roar of many airplanes. Their anticipation mounted, but the planes didn't seem to be getting closer. Then, off in the distance a mile away, they could barely see a thousand tiny figures falling through the clouds and into the trees and swamp.

## NO CLEAR PROLIFERATION

There is nothing that produces more hyperbole and paranoia than nuclear weapons. The order came that C-130 squadrons must have a certain number of crews that were nuclear qualified. Our training was to prepare us to load, unload and handle these top-secret very sensitive instruments of mass destruction.

The class was set up in a small auditorium with armed guards at all entrances. The crew members were required to have top-secret clearance with written orders to attend the training. To enter the class it was necessary to go through two separate stations, each with an access list.

By the time I got to the main room, I felt both privileged and daunted to be trusted with my country's most lethal weapons. On the stage was an atomic bomb on a special dolly. It took a team of eight to load and unload it, including one on each side of the dolly following with wheel chocks on a pole. During practice, I noticed the bomb had a dent about the size of a fist in the front. Something had apparently run into it. It sent a chill up my spine.

Three weeks after becoming nuclear qualified, I got a call from operations to fly an airplane to Ft. Campbell, KY. Upon reporting, I discovered we would be hauling a nuclear weapon. Needless to say, the enormity of the charge hit home. With heightened attention, our crew reviewed the loading and unloading procedures in preparation for handling the nuclear weapon. Arriving at the airplane, although puzzled, we nevertheless were relieved to find our bomb already loaded and tied down.

After landing at Ft. Campbell, we were met by an army sergeant who managed the paperwork to accept the bomb. He informed us that the officers' club was closed and Base Ops would provide us a car for transportation to the enlisted men's mess, where we could eat.

As we got in the car, we could still see our airplane. Amazed, we watched as a truck backed up the airplane ramp, hooked up to the bomb dolly and roared away – a crew of one.

We did not have to puzzle long, because the bomb beat us to

the mess hall. There it was parked in front, still attached to the truck, exposed to the world and now with a crew of zero. The driver was gone. We were dumbfounded, but then we noticed the dent in the bomb. This was the same bomb used in our nuclear training class.

We found the driver eating lunch. When asked what the deal was with the bomb, he answered. "That old bomb is just a teaching aid. It has been declassified for years."

# CHAPTER 6

## CRASH
### (BUT FOR THE GRACE OF GOD)

*A ship is safe in harbor,*
*but that's not what ships are for.*

—WILLIAM G. T. SHEDD

1981: APPROACHING KNOXVILLE, TENNESSEE — There's a saying in aviation: a *mid air* will ruin your whole day.

We were maneuvering at 12,000 feet for an approach at Knoxville's Tyson Field. Our DC-9 was flying through heavy cloud cover with short periods in the clear. Though we were flying on instruments, it was a normal impulse to look up when a break occurred in the clouds.

As we emerged for a brief visual moment – an electric jolt of horror – like the flit of one frame on a movie film – it was there and gone. But I saw it and so did my co-pilot. A twin engine Cessna not 25 feet from my windshield – the frightened face of its pilot as he passed under at a closure rate of 500 knots, so close I was sure it would strike our airplane. But it didn't.

On later communication with approach control I learned that the Cessna pilot was not instrument qualified, and when he attempted to escape the weather, he became disoriented and lost track of his altitude. A small change in our own altitude or descent and we would have spread aluminum all over the Great Smoky Mountains National Park.

This was one of five times in 35 years and 25,000 hours of flying when disaster loomed – when I almost bought the farm. Of course, there were other tense moments, an engine fire, mechanical malfunctions and false warnings, but none of these rose to the level of being life-threatening. And there were tense flying situations when my pulse raced and adrenalin flowed, but that was what made it interesting. I did get shot at a few times, but there are others who are far more qualified to tell the combat stories.

But back to my hair raising times.

1965: SAIGON, SOUTH VIETNAM — I arrived for the first time at Saigon's Tan Son Nhut airport in the spring of 1965. It was a madhouse. Most of the Vietnam flying during this time was classified as tactical emergencies. The U.S. military had begun a massive buildup and the attending chaos was everywhere. The small international airport was overwhelmed. In a few short months it would become the busiest airport in the world.

I was the aircraft commander of a crew of five on a C-130. In this caldron of confusion we had been assigned three weeks of flying duty in South Vietnam. The C-130s were affectionately called *trash haulers,* because we hauled anything and everything.

Early afternoon found us at Pleiku Air Base in the central highlands. This base had a strong military presence to stop the enemy infiltration from neighboring Cambodia and Laos. Our mission was to deliver a desperately needed trailer tank of potable water to a temporary landing field located close to the Laotian border.

Using the TACAN navigation radio to gauge direction and distance, we let down to 5,000 feet. To the west was a small airfield cut out of the jungle with a temporary runway made of interlocking pierced steel plank called PSP. A small wooden shack stood nearby. In the middle of the strip was a jeep with nobody around. About two thirds down from the approach end was an M-48 Patton tank with its 90-mm cannon pointed toward the landing end of the runway.

I had been instructed to view the field from a distance, and if things looked okay, make a pass at 2,000 feet to get a flashing green light for landing clearance. With the equipment on the runway, it was obvious we could not land, but we flew over anyway to announce our arrival. As soon as our flyover began, somebody stepped out of the shack and flashed the green light, as if all that was required was a nice green light to attract us to our spot like a mating lightning bug. We ignored the light and made another pass. This time a soldier went out and moved the jeep. Nobody attempted to move the tank. After two more passes, each time receiving the green light, it became obvious the tank was inoperable.

We now seriously contemplated landing using only the first two thirds of the runway. Calculating our stopping distance, I tried to estimate how much runway remained between the approach end of the PSP and the tank. This was a guess, since I didn't know how much was there with no tank. Something else we didn't know: a heavy thunderstorm had been over the area, and the ground beneath the PSP runway was saturated with water.

Normally, this whole mission would be against regulations, but we were operating under a tactical emergency – which, in essence, meant we could do whatever we had nerve enough to do.

With the agreement of my co-pilot, I decided an assault landing would work. An assault landing is an effective but violent way to terminate a flight. Some called it a controlled crash. No attempt is made for a smooth touchdown. The idea is to hit an exact spot at a high rate of descent at the slowest safe flying speed. The hard landing dissipates part of the momentum of the aircraft and shortens the landing roll. To execute this requires the simultaneous application of a 100-percent reverse thrust and maximum wheel braking at the instant of impact. When done well, the landing roll is amazingly short. I had practiced many assault landings and I was good at them.

Still, not knowing the length of available runway added risk, but adding unknown braking conditions to the mix was a recipe for disaster. But we were young and cocky, and this was war.

I hit the very end of the landing strip at minimum flying speed, with 1,500 feet per minute descent. I was hyped. The props were in full reverse on touchdown – *excellent*. On impact I went to max braking. But nothing. Mud came up through the PSP, turning it eel-skin slick. The anti-skid cycled continuously, indicating no braking. The reverse thrust of the big Hamilton Standard propellers sucked up mud and water and within seconds we were engulfed in a huge cloud. It marked our race with death toward the tank. We could not see beyond our instruments. There was no way to tell our ever decreasing distance from the Patton tank.

I held my breath expecting disaster. Given the position of the gun, I knew it would act like a can opener and puncture and obliterate whatever hit it. But suddenly, we stopped, the giant cloud dissipated, and I was staring at the 90-mm cannon not five feet from my face. The co-pilot looked at me with wide, dilated eyes – neither of us could speak. A small variation in our touchdown, the rate of descent or timing, and that gun would have been in our cockpit.

We unloaded the water and prepared to return to Tan Son Nhut. Two soldiers released for R&R had planned to catch our plane to Saigon. After watching our arrival, however, they declined the ride.

1966: REPUBLIC OF SOUTH VIETNAM — A basic principal of aviation, which cannot be ignored, even in war: the vacuum created by the camber of an airplane wing is generated by the air rushing across it. This vacuum can be measured in pounds. When the pounds of the airplane and its cargo exceed the pounds of generated vacuum, the airplane will not fly – it crashes.

Fifteen miles east of Kon Tum airfield, a raging battle was in progress with North Vietnamese regulars. It was not going well. We received an emergency call for airlift and headed to the small Kon Tum field to move unspecified fighting equipment to Pleiku.

As I surveyed the situation, an army staff sergeant approached. He looked tired and stressed and gave a half-hearted salute that looked more like a wave. What barely passed as a uniform was dirty and wet with sweat.

I asked if we could be of assistance in moving his equipment. He pointed to a three-axle truck, the kind with the high chuck wagon canvas top. Fastened to the hitch on the truck was a 105-mm Howitzer cannon on wheels. He had been ordered to get it all to Pleiku as soon as possible.

When I inquired about the weight, the sergeant said the truck was 20,000 pounds and the gun another 15,000 pounds. Taking into account runway length, elevation and temperature, I made some calculations and told him we could take the Howitzer or the truck but not both. With a look more of desperation than disappointment, he insisted both had to go, the battle depended on it. I recalculated, using all the fudge factor that I dared. *There was no way – I could only take off with a maximum cargo of 25,000 lbs.* I told him again, either the truck or the gun but not both. As he turned to discuss the problem with another sergeant, I got the impression he didn't believe me. I guess he thought, *hey man, they don't call this airplane the C-130 Hercules for nothing.* But he didn't comment.

With obvious reluctance, they decided to take the truck without the gun.

As the truck drove up our back ramp, I became uneasy. The truck seemed to require high power settings, even in the lowest gear, and as it proceeded into the cargo hold, the airplane settled ominously lower. I got a sick feeling: *something was wrong.*

I walked up the ramp to the truck and moved the canvas. Stacked five feet high were wooden boxes. "Sergeant, what is this?"

Sheepishly, "That's the gun ammunition, sir."

"How much does it weigh?"

"Sir, I don't know exactly but about 20,000 pounds. When you said you could take the truck, I figured you could take what was in it."

"Were you going to accompany your truck to Pleiku?"

"Yes, sir."

"Sergeant, nobody would have made it to Pleiku. You, along with the rest of us, would have died in flames at the end of the Kom Tum runway. It would have been a spectacular ball of fire fed by JP-4 fuel and 20,000 pounds of 105-mm Howitzer ammunition."

1990: ARRIVAL AT THE GATE IN DALLAS (DFW) — Could a small boy cause a Delta jumbo jet to crash, even before it took off?

Most aircraft accidents are caused by the occurrence of a series of failures culminating into disaster.

Disaster step one: arriving at the gate in Dallas, we shut down the second engine of the Boeing 767. A minor electrical problem developed as our auxiliary power unit tried to pick up the power load. After a brief discussion with the line mechanic, we concluded it would correct itself once the engine was restarted and power transferred back to the engine generator.

Disaster step two: our intermediate stop lasted about 45 minutes. The co-pilot and I got out of our seats and stood around in the first class galley chatting with the flight attendants. Meanwhile, a mechanic sat in the left seat to do some routine maintenance checks.

Disaster step three: a boy appeared at the cockpit entrance. The mechanic, being of good nature, invited the lad to sit in the other pilot seat. This was not unusual. After answering several questions, the mechanic picked up the logbook to record his checks. The boy continued holding the yoke and occasionally touched some of the fascinating knobs and instruments. Two knobs that fascinated him were the engine throttles.

When the mechanic's work was done, both he and the boy left the cockpit. The mechanic proceeded to the tug attached to the airplane nose wheel, the boy to his cabin seat.

Disaster step four: the co-pilot and I took our cockpit seats; I called for the *intermediate* stop checklist.

Normal procedure was for the tug to push back the airplane prior to engine start. The tug would then disconnect and leave.

At this gate, we were pushed back just enough to clear the terminal on our turn for the taxiway.

As the first engine came up to speed, instead of watching it stabilize at idle, both the co-pilot and I looked at the overhead electrical panel to see if the power did indeed transfer. Neither of us saw the engine continue to wind up to 100 percent thrust instead of idle. Our first clue was the surging of the aircraft – and a loud roar, quickly followed by the frantic calls from the mechanic.

The Boeing 767 has two General Electric CF-56 engines, each of which produces more than 60,000 pounds of thrust. They are capable of launching a 400,000 pound airplane. Because of our minor electrical problem, I had asked the mechanic to leave the tug attached and stay on the intercom until we were sure our power would transfer on engine start. The airplane brakes alone could not hold. Had the tug not still been attached with its brakes locked, the jumbo jet could have been hurtled into the Dallas-Fort Worth terminal.

*Note: This was my mistake. Instead of the intermediate, I should have run the full checklist. This would have caught the throttles at full power. We also would have caught it on engine start if we had not been looking overhead.*

1985: HIGH ALTITUDE APPROACH AT CHICAGO O'HARE — Chicago, along with Atlanta, has the finest controllers in the world. The sector center, approach control, and tower will all get it right – or will they?

by Chicago center to intercept the instrument landing system for runway 31 left and descend to 15,000 feet. It was unusual to intercept the localizer so far out, but it made sense because our position put us almost on it already, and the localizer signal was strong. We also received the glide slope and descended on it at about 450 knots ground speed.

Our center controller was due a break so he swapped out with a new controller. The new controller thought we had been switched to approach control. On initial contact with approach control, the airplanes were given a speed reduction. Since we were not switched to approach, we did not get our speed reduction. Due to speed differences, we were closing on the airplane in front at about 150 knots. As we progressed, we could hear the new controller directing traffic behind us, but we no longer heard flights in front being switched over to approach. Maybe we had lost radio contact.

My co-pilot picked up the mic to inquire as we broke out of the clouds. "Look out," he screamed – I was already making a hard bank to avoid running up the tail of another Boeing 727.

Were it not for that momentary break in the clouds, we would have collided.

Young pilots think when they hear of an aviation disaster that it wouldn't happen to them. They would have had the skill – *the right stuff.* Old pilots think, *There, but for the grace of God go I.*

# CHAPTER 7
## FREUD

### (FLYING REPRESENTS EARLY UGLY DEATH)

*Fear makes the wolf bigger than he is.*

—(GERMAN PROVERB)

1992: ATLANTA (ATL), GEORGIA — Flight 242 from Atlanta to Houston was boarding 15 minutes late. With growing anxiety, my 23-year-old daughter glanced into the cockpit. The pilots looked nervous. And the flight attendants, she could tell, were keeping something from her. She found her seat and buckled herself in. As the Delta jet pushed back from the gate, she could hear a whining noise in the belly of the airplane. She was sure of it – this airplane was going to crash. She unlatched her seatbelt, grabbed her bag and ran up the aisle to the flight attendant, demanding to get off the plane. Clutched in her hand was my employee pass.

After 40 years of flying airplanes, I don't have a good explanation for why some people are relaxed when flying, and others think they are about to die. The latter sort, the one I call Flying Represents Early Ugly Death or FREUD, is the group to which my daughter belongs. No matter that her father was a pilot and she had flown from the time she was a baby without difficulty or incident. But sometime around her 18th birthday, her phobia took hold. She was not alone – her mother also suffered from FREUD.

All airplanes make a variety of noises. There is the changing tone of the engines, the intermittent high-pitched scream from hydraulic pumps and the rush of air through ducts. A pronounced thump can usually be heard when the landing gear comes up or down, and the ever-present wind noise varies with speed changes. Occasionally, passengers close to the front can hear sounds of bells and horns from the cockpit. Most passengers disregard these sounds – but FREUDs fixate on them and imagine each sound is a harbinger of death.

Flying time on a commercial airline today is actually safer than when not flying. But I learned years ago that citing statistics to a FREUD was pointless. It's like telling an arachnophobic that spiders are our friends. Once, while I was deadheading in uniform to cover a trip, a flight attendant asked if I would try to calm a FREUD. Approaching the woman, I could plainly see her distress. When she realized I was coming to sit down next to her, she looked at me as if I were an ax-murderer with the bloody weapon in my hand. In an attempt to calm her, I thought I would explain the various movements and sounds related to taxiing and takeoff and do so in a gentle, but matter-of-fact way. Patting myself on the back for my psychology, I continued this monologue for a half an hour – her silence affirmation of the effectiveness of my approach. At least I thought it was until we hit an air bump and she gripped the armrest like it was her last hold on life, mouth open and eyes blazing like the face in Edvard Munch's painting of *The Scream*.

The behavior of FREUDS can be erratic. Sometimes they evidence no fear of flying. And in other contexts, they are often not anxious people. But it's useful to recognize that for a FREUD terror is there, lurking just below the surface, ready to strike without warning.

In 1966, I lived in Okinawa with my first wife, Nancy. We had three small children, and, due to the war, I spent most of my time in Southeast Asia. While not pleased with the arrangement, Nancy, at 25, nonetheless took it in stride. On one occasion while I was away, she and the children endured a typhoon that hit the island and lingered for 36 hours. It dumped 15 inches of rain, causing a mudslide that came through our house. Through it all, Nancy tended to the children and kept her cool.

When we returned to the United States, Northwest Airlines flew us to San Francisco with a stop in Tokyo. During the climb out from Tokyo, the Boeing 707 suddenly leveled off, and we heard a thud accompanied with a slight jolt in the aircraft. I recognized it as the landing gear cycling down and then back up. This procedure often will clear a faulty light indication of an unsafe gear.

I was about to say something, but Nancy was already sobbing. The more I tried to explain, the more she was convinced that our children would never see America because we were descending to a watery grave. Neighboring passengers looked concerned. I wondered what they must be thinking, taking in the scene of a man in an Air Force uniform unable to console the distressed woman. A flight attendant attempted to calm my wife, but failing, went to get the captain.

I cringed, embarrassed that I, a uniformed pilot, was unable to manage the situation. I did the only thing that made sense to me at the time – I pretended I didn't know who she was. That plan, however, was foiled when my daughter, upset over her mother, climbed onto my lap and called me Daddy.

It took some doing, but the captain finally convinced Nancy that if there were a problem, he would be in the cockpit fighting for our lives, rather than talking to her.

Nancy's reaction on our Northwest flight was not without precedent. On an earlier occasion, we had gone on a much-needed vacation without the children and were flying standby on a C-130 cargo airplane. We had been to Baguio City in the Philippines and were trying to make our way back to Okinawa. Our plane made a stop in Taipei to pick up cargo. It was common for military personnel to order furniture custom-made in Taipei. When a C-130 passed through on a cargo run, if space was available, this furniture would be loaded for transport to Okinawa. On this particular flight, so much furniture had been loaded there was barely enough room for me, my wife and the two military enlisted men traveling standby with us.

C-130s are not comfortable airplanes for passengers. The seats are made of webbing and fold down from the side walls. All models are loud, but the A model we were flying was even more so. There are no windows, just small portholes. For some reason, the loadmaster loaded the cargo compartment in such a way that the only seats were behind a giant stack of furniture that went all the way to the ceiling, which on this plane was very high.

After a short passenger briefing, we crawled in behind the furniture to the four web seats located about the middle of the fuselage. I was seated to Nancy's left, and the two soldiers were on her right.

During takeoff and through the first part of our trip, Nancy showed some apprehension, but most passengers would under the rough conditions. About 45 minutes before arrival at Naha Air Base in Okinawa, the aircraft yawed slightly, and the propeller sound changed. All eyes turned to me for an explanation. I had to shout to be heard, yelling that the props had momentarily gotten out of synchronization but everything was fine. The soldiers accepted this and relaxed, but Nancy was not buying it. She glanced around the aircraft like a trapped animal. All of a sudden, screaming, she grabbed my arm and pointed to the porthole behind us. Much to my surprise, I could see the number three engine propeller was not turning. Clearly, my prior assessment was incorrect. With a wife on the verge of hysteria and the two soldiers with alarm in their eyes, I tried to explain that this was not really serious and we often practiced flying and even landed on three engines. The soldiers were only partially listening to me while looking at my upset wife – I could see I had lost some credibility.

After about 20 minutes, everyone became calmer, but as our pilots reduced power and started the descent for landing, apprehension started to build again.

The main runway at Naha had two approaches – one over land and the other over water. We had different procedures for briefing the passengers, depending on the landing direction. Because of the loud flight conditions, this briefing was usually made before departure. If an approach was scheduled over water the passengers were issued life vests and were required to wear them. When we departed Taipei, evidently the planned approach was over land, because no life vests had been issued. Now, because of the engine situation, our approach would be made over water, which meant the passengers needed to wear their life vests.

Without warning the loadmaster appeared over the top of the furniture, he was shouting and waving his arms. Nancy and the terrified solders looked up at him like he was the grim reaper. Slinging life vests at us, he yelled, "PUT ON YOUR LIFE VESTS! PUT ON YOUR LIFE VESTS!"

I started to explain the part about the required overwater landing procedure. Frantically getting into their life vests as if it were the one small chance they now had of survival, the three of them ignored me. Braced for a crash into the ocean, they were utterly amazed when we landed smoothly and taxied to the ramp.

*Note: My second wife is also named Nancy. There is nothing in this story that refers to her. She is not a FREUD. But on land, my foot barely crosses the threshold before the door is locked behind me. She sees danger around every corner – but she is not afraid of flying. Go figure.*

# PART 4

DELTA AIR LINES

# CHAPTER 8
## THE MISSING CAPTAIN

*Experience is a dear teacher,*
*and only fools will learn from no other.*

—BENJAMIN FRANKLIN

1970: HOUSTON (IAH) TEXAS — Bob Norris was legendary on the airline. Although he was an excellent pilot, his fame came not from his flying but from his practical jokes. Being a bit of a jokester myself, I was pleased to be paired with Bob as his co-pilot.

Bob was young for a captain, but his flying experience was extensive. His father had run a fixed base operation, and he started flying at the age of 15, which made it possible for him to qualify for his aviation ratings at the minimum ages. He was tall and thin like a coyote that had not eaten for a week. He walked with a slight swagger, his captain's hat pushed back and a hint of a smile, as if something was up and he knew, but you didn't.

Our two-day trip flying the DC-9 started in Houston and we were on the ground in Chicago on the second day. There, we were scheduled to pick up Houston-based flight attendants, who would work with us the next two legs from Chicago to Memphis, and on to our home base in Houston. While boarding, we learned the attendants were new, on the third and last day of their first Delta rotation. Bob shot me a knowing look.

Since Chicago's O'Hare Field typically has a long taxi time before takeoff, the flight attendant working up front was able to complete her work and had time to come to the cockpit. I don't know what jokes or lies she had been exposed to the previous two days, but in an effort to not act like a new hire with us, she adopted an attitude that was as affected as it was rude. It is difficult to fake being an experienced flight attendant.

She bounced into the cockpit reeking of bravado. "What's happening, guys?"

With a slight smile, Bob turned to look at her. "I'm Bob Norris. This is Steve Taylor. You want to tell us your name?"

"So you're Captain Norris, I've heard about you."

"Well, I hope it's been good."

"Nope, it's all bad."

"Am I going to make up a name for you, or do you have one you would like to use?"

"It's Pidd Cook, P-I-D-D. What's it to you?"

Bob smiled again as if he knew something she didn't. "Well, I may need to contact you. It would be better if I didn't have to just say, hey you working first class."

Evidently Pidd was unaware that, as the lead flight attendant, she was required to introduce herself to the captain.

"Well," she said, "don't give me any lip about it or you won't get anything to drink." And with that, she left the cockpit.

"What do you make of Pidd?" I asked Bob.

"I think maybe we need to take her down a notch or two," he replied.

The DC-9 had a trap door in the cockpit floor that was hard to distinguish from the metal floor around it. The door led to an area that contained electronic equipment with enough room inside for a mechanic to work.

Once we hit cruise on the way to Houston, Bob opened the trap door, entered the compartment, and closed the door behind him. I rang the flight attendant call button and Pidd answered. "Hey, what can I do you for?"

"Pidd, would you come to the cockpit for a minute?"

"Watcha want? I'm busy," she said, sticking her head in the cockpit.

"The company called and they want to talk with Captain Norris. Would you get him back up here?"

Pidd left to find Bob. Some minutes later she returned more serious than before. "I can't find him."

"This is important," I said. "You didn't look hard enough. He must be in the lavatory in the back or visiting with a passenger. Go find him now!"

This time she left without making a smart remark.

When she returned next she looked frightened. She came into the cockpit and closed the door behind her. "Steve, I can't find him. I have looked in all the seats and in all the lavatories. He is not on this airplane."

"You – ah – don't suppose we left him in Memphis?"

"Left him? How could you leave the captain?"

"I . . . I don't know. I guess I just got busy and didn't notice."

"I . . . I don't understand! Can you land without him?"

"I don't know. I guess I'll have to try. The one thing we don't want is for anybody else to know the danger here. I am going to be very busy. You need to go back, and don't bother me unless I ring for you – and don't say a word about this to anybody."

By now she was pale and looked like she was about to cry. She uttered a weak, "Yes, sir," and left.

I tapped on the trap door and Bob came out and took his seat. Just before starting our descent for landing, I rang for Pidd to come up.

When she entered and saw Bob in his seat, her eyes widened, but before she could say anything, he asked her for a cup of coffee.

"What – where have you been? What's going on?"

Calmly, Bob said, "What do you mean? I have been right here the whole flight."

"Unh-uh, you've done something – I don't understand."

Once again Bob asked for his coffee. She left and returned with the coffee, handed it to him and departed without saying anything else.

After landing, Pidd returned to the cockpit to report that one of the coffee makers was not working, her officious demeanor restored.

Bob, in an irritated tone, said, "I cannot record that in the log book. It is unsafe to fly with an inoperable coffeemaker. Didn't you read the safety bulletin on that coffee maker before you came on this trip? That is part of your professional responsibilities to read the bulletin board."

"I di-didn't know – are you sure?"

"Of course I'm sure. You surely didn't try to use it?"

"I think . . . I think . . . I might have."

"You're lucky you didn't cause a fire. From now on be sure to perform your preflight duties before you come on board."

"Yes, sir."

After we landed and Pidd had finished all her duties with our final flight, I watched her cut a bee-line to the flight attendant lounge to read the safety items on the bulletin board. But Bob Norris did not get his reputation by not finalizing his jokes. He had left the airplane soon after we arrived at the gate and went to operations to secure paper with an official letterhead. When Pidd arrived at the bulletin board there was the phony safety memo about the fire hazard from faulty coffee makers.

A variation of the disappearing act was played on a subsequent flight when Bob Norris was flying with co-pilot Ted Thomas. In this case it was Ted who disappeared into the equipment area.

While Bob and Ted were having a friendly argument, Molly, the first class flight attendant, thought they were actually mad at each other and tried to lower the hostility. Bob recognized that she was a peacemaker and created a plan to exploit this trait.

When Captain Norris was away from Ted, he would tell Molly how despicable his co-pilot was, and when Ted was alone with her, he would talk about how he hated the captain. All the time, Molly kept insisting that neither of them was bad, and they shouldn't say these ugly things.

While on the ground at a stopover in Jackson, Mississippi, Captain Norris went out to the ticket counter to talk with Molly, who was discussing something with the agent during boarding. He pulled her to one side and complained, "That co-pilot went somewhere and has not returned. He is neglecting his work. I am thinking of throwing him off the flight."

"But there is no pilot base in Jackson. How could we get another co-pilot?" Molly said.

"He is worthless anyhow. I'm already doing all the work."

"He will be back soon. We have a few minutes yet," pleaded Molly.

"Well, if he doesn't show up by departure, I'm leaving him."

Bob walked back to the cockpit and closed the door. Ted quickly opened the trap door and entered the equipment compartment. Captain Norris reopened the cockpit door and got in his seat to prepare for taxi. When departure time came, he turned and shouted to Molly, "Close the cabin door. We're leaving without him."

"But we can't leave without a co-pilot." By now Molly was standing in the cockpit looking very anxious.

"Yes, we can! Close the door and let's go."

She weakly motioned for the agent to close the cabin door. When it was closed and secure, Bob turned and asked her to come back to the cockpit. "When you leave, I want you to close the cockpit door, and don't come back up here until we get to Shreveport. I'm going to be too busy to talk."

As soon as the cockpit door was closed and locked, Captain Norris rapped on the trap door for Ted to come out. Molly, as instructed, steered clear of the cockpit during the flight.

On taxi in to the gate in Shreveport, Ted went back into the equipment compartment. As soon as the airplane stopped at the gate, he opened a second trap door that led to the outside, jumped to the ramp, closed the door, and ran up the jet-way stairs to arrive outside the main cabin door before it was opened.

Molly took her position at the main cabin door and when it was opened she was confronted with the disheveled co-pilot, tie lose shirt tail half out and a distressed look on his face. "Why did you leave me? I had to run all the way from Jackson."

# CHAPTER 9
## I LOVE NEW YORK

*New York is like a disco,*
*but without the music.*

—ELAINE STRITCH

1973: LAGUARDIA (LGA), NEW YORK — As usual, LaGuardia was swamped with traffic, and our air traffic controller was abrasive. He talked in spurts with a strong Brooklyn accent that I only partially understood. I noticed other pilots were asking him to repeat instructions. The more they asked, the more abrasive and condescending he became. Finally, after his next bombardment of directives, delivered with machine-gun rapidity, I said in my slowest Southern drawl: "LaGuardia . . . this- is- Delta- 482 . . . . Do- you- hear- how- fast- I- am- talking?"

"Roger that, Delta."

"Well . . . that's- how- fast- I- listen."

I knew what he wanted to say, but he didn't dare. He did slow it down.

Delta had recently completed a merger with Northeast Airlines and eliminated most of the unions that were so strong on Northeast. There were many malcontented ground workers at LaGuardia Airport who had lost union representation, making an already disagreeable bunch even more disagreeable. So it had been a long day of flying as first officer on a Convair 880, and I was looking forward to a pastrami sandwich and beer.

With the rest of the crew, I checked into the New York Park Sheraton on 7th Avenue for a 16-hour layover. Upon learning that the captain and I were going next door to the famous Carnegie Deli, one of our flight attendants asked me to bring her back a sandwich. I changed my clothes and met the captain in the hotel lobby.

It had been a year since I'd been in New York, and I was

struggling to adjust my temperament to take on the locals. Even though I was looking forward to the food, I was not looking forward to the accompanying attitude of the deli staff, which famously warns all customers in its marketing: "Don't expect to make friends with the wait staff. This is NYC, you order food, food is served, you eat food, you pay, you leave. Life is fast here and no one wants to slow down."

I have to admit, while growing up in Charleston during the 40s and 50s, I had a distaste for Yankees in general. Along with the stories about Yankees stealing livestock and burning farms during the war of Northern aggression, the history I learned in my small Southern school emphasized the evils of Carpetbaggers, Scalawags and Reconstruction. I can't say I actually knew any Yankees while growing up, but they still left a bad taste in my mouth.

At age 13, I was hitchhiking on Savannah Highway to a friend's house. It was spring, and New Yorkers were driving the Ocean Highway north from Miami. There was no chance they would stop to pick up hitchhikers in South Carolina. I kept a few rocks in my hand, and when a car appeared with a New York license plate, instead of holding up my thumb, I would launch a rock. One time, I heard a loud crack as my rock hit a big Cadillac. It squealed to a stop and backed up. I decided to stand my ground and see what would happen. The driver jumped out and seemed somewhat taken aback because I did not run. He said I had cracked his windshield and wanted to know why.

"Sir, I can see from your license plate you are a Yankee, and knew you would not give me a ride. I am sorry about your windshield."

Confused, he got back in his car and left. I might add that I was cocked to run for the woods at any moment.

I admit to blind unjustified prejudice against Yankees in my youth, but by the time of my layover in New York, I had been to a lot of places and had known many a good Yankee and actually came to like a few of them. But I still was not ready for one of those *I love New York* t-shirts. And so it was that I entered the Carnegie Deli with my captain. We sat down at a community table with two New Yorkers gorging on immense piles of meat, and waited for the big hairy-armed waiter to insult us over how or what we chose to eat.

While we waited, I decided to order the flight attendant's sandwich and made my way to the takeout line. When my turn came, before I could say a word, the burly staffer behind the counter said, "Are yuse sitting at ah table?"

"Yes, but I need . . ."

"Yuse can't order from here."

"But I'm ordering take . . ."

"I told yah. I ain't takin' no order to da tables."

By now all my effort to adjust my attitude failed. My face reddened, and I raised my voice several decibels. "Listen, you fool, I'm trying to order takeout and . . ."

Meanwhile a derelict wandered in from the street and went over to my captain, hit him hard on the arm and said, "You don't like black people do you?"

The captain caught the eye of the manager and motioned for him to come over. As the manager made his way, the derelict strayed in the direction where I was then loudly venting my frustration.

The captain pointed at the stray just as he was passing near me and said, "That guy is causing trouble. He just came over and hit me."

The next thing I knew I was grabbed by the shirt collar and pants and was given the bum's rush out the door. From the sidewalk where I landed, I could hear the captain explain to the manager that he had gotten the wrong man. The manager apologized and invited me back in.

He was both relieved and surprised that I found the whole thing exceedingly funny. Then he, too, found it funny. Yes, New Yorkers do laugh. I still won't wear the shirt, but I will say this: in my own peculiar way – *I love New York* – or at least I love to hate it.

# CHAPTER 10

## HOUSE OF HORRORS

*Where there is no imagination there is no horror.*

—SIR ARTHUR CONAN DOYLE

1971: HOUSTON, TEXAS — About 10:15 p.m., I heard a loud rapid knock on my door along with the continuous ringing of the doorbell. When I answered, Herb blurted, "My house's being robbed! They're still there. Get your gun."

I grabbed my .45, although, unknown to Herb, it wasn't loaded. We quietly entered his house, my gun in the ready position. Proceeding from room to room like characters in a TV cop show, I strained to stifle my laughter. Finally Herb declared, "They must've heard us when we came in through the back door and left after we ran out."

He called his wife, who had gone next door to Carolyn's house.

Carolyn came over with Gayle and the four of us started through the house to survey the loss. Herb and Gayle argued and stepped on each other's story about who had run first when they thought they were interrupting a burglary.

According to Herb: "We entered together through the back door, and when I saw the sheet on the floor with the silver, I instantly concluded we were being robbed. It looked like they were still in the house, so I told Gayle to run while I followed her back out."

According to Gayle: "Herb entered first through the back door and I followed behind him. He saw the sheet, screamed, and ran over me, pushing me out of the way, as he panicked to escape."

They argued about this while the four of us proceeded into the living room, noting the only thing missing was a single picture. Gayle had claimed on several occasions that the picture was very valuable, and now, with a hint of satisfaction, she announced,

"They're professionals. They were only interested in the most valuable items. They know what they're doing."

Trying to control her laughter, Carolyn looked out the window; I looked at the floor.

We proceeded up the stairs where I had placed an empty leather gun case that had held Herb's most prized gun. "Well, they got my guns," Herb grunted in disgust.

I looked at the floor again.

Gayle's pace increased as we approached the closet where her sewing machine was kept. Carolyn looked at me knowingly. Then we heard what we had never heard before come from Gayle's mouth: "Shit, they took my sewing machine."

This was all we could bear; Carolyn and I burst out laughing. Herb looked confused, "What's so damn funny about . . . what's going on . . . we've been . . . is this some kind of joke? . . . Honey, we've been had."

Although Gayle did not think anything about the prank was funny, she was so relieved that she had not been robbed that she agreed with all of us to have a "didn't-rob-my-house party." We invited some more neighbors and the party went on until 1 a.m.

It did not go unnoticed by me that during our didn't-rob-my-house-party, Herb stated several times that the great deception would not go unpunished. The joke escalation had begun.

It all started in 1971 when I lived on a quiet cul-de-sac in Inverness Forest, a subdivision 20 miles north of Houston, Texas. To the left of my house was the home of another Delta pilot, Ron Davis, and to the left of him lived a hard-charging, upwardly mobile IBM salesman by the name of Herb Hern. We were all about the same age and had become friends. The three of us hunted together, drank beer together, visited and gave each other advice on various backyard projects. We were competitive and aggressive.

Our planned deer hunt for the fall in far west Texas had become a competition by some of the hunters for bragging rights to arrive at hunt camp with the "baddest" off-road vehicle. Herb had purchased a new four-wheel drive Blazer; however, at our first hunt meeting at Ron's house, Herb was ridiculed as having a lady's carpool van. Ron announced that he had ordered a new Ford off-road pickup that would put them all to shame. He had some pictures, and it did look impressive. It had oversized lug tires and was jacked up so high that it should have come with a ladder to climb into what Ron called the cockpit. It appeared he was preparing for a hunt on a muddy 45-degree incline strewn with three-foot boulders. Obviously, he was pleased with the impression it made, as the others present talked less about their own macho machines.

It should be noted that I was not competing in the vehicle contest, but the following year I aced them all by being the only one to show up with a horse. At this time, however, I was envious of them and their monster trucks. I was feeding four rug monsters at home and did not yet have the earning power.

Ron took delivery of his jacked up, four-wheel drive, terrain traverser four months before our hunt. He and Bob Norris, another Delta pilot on our hunt, took the truck to Bob's farm outside of Palestine, Texas. Sometime while they were riding around, the end of a piece of wire pierced the seal on the differential, and over time the fluid drained, causing severe damage.

Ron had bragged so much about his off-road Ford that he received unending ridicule about his big tough truck that looked good on the highway, but broke as soon as it left the road. He called the dealer and complained bitterly. After a long conversation with the maintenance shop, they convinced him that his problem was an odd, one-time thing. The dealer installed a new differential, and Ron accepted the return of his truck.

Once he got his truck back home, Ron was undeterred and continued crowing about its capabilities. Not being in the *mean truck* competition, I thought the whole thing was silly, and that they all needed a dose of humility – Ron most of all.

Since Macho Truck was made for tough outside work, it was always parked on the driveway. It probably would not even have fit in the garage. Unless he was going somewhere with his wife, he always drove his truck. All of Houston was a rough outback to be conquered, but there was always the slight nagging doubt for which he had been thoroughly ridiculed – *It looks good on the highway, but it will break as soon as it leaves the pavement.*

Ron had already explained in painful detail that he had discovered an oil stain on his driveway about the time his differential failed. I couldn't resist: I went by the auto shop and got some gear oil and a squirt can. Just before I went to bed, I sneaked over to Ron's driveway and crawled under his Macho Truck. I squirted the gear oil on top of the differential so that it not only appeared on the hub as if it were leaking, but over time, it would pool underneath on the driveway where it would be seen.

I did this three nights in a row, and on the fourth night the truck was gone. I found out the next day that Ron had called the dealer and said, "You can come and get this son-of-a-bitch piece of junk, and I never want to see it again."

Later, Ron retrieved his truck when he learned he had been tricked. He vowed to get even. But I guess the joke tempo really started to intensify when Carolyn Roberts and I staged the fake robbery on Herb's house. Carolyn was the fourth neighbor on the cul-de-sac. She was saucy and had a better sense of humor than the other wives. Her husband declined to get involved with the faked robbery, stating that we would find ourselves on the bad side of Herb's wife, which has already been shown we did.

Gayle was very prim and proper. She had already indicated she did not appreciate the humor in our small jokes and criticized us if our language turned salty.

In July, I went on a two-week vacation with my family. When I returned home I noticed a scornful look from two of my neighbors. I waved; they did not wave back, and as I drew closer to my house there were several young boys circling the cul-de-sac on their bikes and laughing. Then I saw it: In my overgrown yard the word "FUCK" was mowed in huge letters.

I ran to start my lawn mower, even before I unloaded the car, but it was too late. *The Word* had been there long enough that everybody knew about it, and it was scheduled to be discussed in a subdivision committee meeting the next day. Most people were not impressed with my explanation and thought I was some sort of pervert. Herb told his wife that the other Delta pilot, Ron Davis, had mowed it there. She was quick to accept this because she was convinced that all pilots had flawed personalities.

Through some forensic investigation, I determined Herb was the culprit. First off, Ron had a yard service and did not own a lawnmower. There were, also, some cut marks that were consistent with Herb's mower. He would not admit it and even pretended that he thought Ron had done it, but he knew that I knew.

I could not let this go unaddressed, so the plan for my retaliation began. My opportunity came in August when Herb and his family went to visit his mother-in-law for the weekend.

I was quite proud of my stereo system, which I had built from a kit. One feature I especially liked was using the microphone to talk through my speakers. At Halloween, I put the speakers in trees to scare the trick-or-treaters.

So now I ran a speaker wire from my amplifier out through my fireplace chimney, through the trees at Ron Davis' house, and over to the top of the fireplace chimney at Herb's house. I dropped the speaker wire down through Herb's chimney, and using the key I had to his house, I entered with an 8 x 12-inch speaker. I lodged the speaker in the top of fireplace with the fireplace damper.

Herb and his family had been home several days before I put my plan into action. I did not want him to associate what was about to occur with me being in his house while he was gone. I got up at 2 a.m. and proceeded in the dark to my stereo set. Keying the mic, I let out a blood-curdling groan that sounded like one of those

Civil War movies, where the soldier is having his leg amputated with no anesthetic. The groan lasted about 30 seconds and it was not repeated.

At Herb's house the lights came on upstairs, then downstairs. Herb investigated downstairs. A few minutes later Gayle joined him. Eventually, they turned off the downstairs lights.

I saw Herb the following day, but nothing was said about the horror the night before. I later found out that they had agreed not to talk about it because, even though they both had heard it, they were not too sure of what they had heard, since it occurred while they were in a deep sleep. If they told the story, people would think they were crazy, barring any evidence of anything physical that was related to the groan.

I went on a Delta trip, but I did not repeat the horror sounds until several days had passed after my return. I then set my watch for 3 a.m. and repeated the same program. During the next two weeks I did this several more times, with some variation, and neither Herb nor Gayle said a word about their habit of roaming the house in the middle of the night. They were, however, looking a little detached and tired.

During the previous episode, after giving out my usual long, tortured, man-in-pain sound, I repeated it once more when the lights went back out. The lights immediately came back on and Herb quickly reappeared downstairs. I thought this action entertaining, so I followed the same routine again. However, this time, after Herb turned out the lights, he did not go back to bed but sat in the dark in his den not ten feet from the fireplace. Herb confessed to me later that when he heard the groaning so close, he almost peed his pants.

The next day Herb presented my speaker. Although he was somewhat triumphant to have ended his ordeal, he was not in a jovial mood. He had suffered a severe tongue lashing from Gayle about his childish pranks and his insane friends. He asked for his house key back and said we must call a truce to save his marriage. They both had lost sleep, but Gayle had trouble going to sleep at all. Only after he had promised to get to the bottom of the noise did she relinquish her demand to go to her mother's house. Although neither of them was superstitious, in the dead of night, it was easy to imagine the house could be haunted.

I apologized that I had upset Gayle, but because I knew she had maligned me repeatedly, secretly, I was delighted.

Our truce lasted several months and we remained friends. Even Gayle began to lighten up and became friendly again. But one Saturday when I was working on my car, Herb regressed. While I went to the auto parts store, I left the hood open, and Herb came over to see how I was doing. When he discovered I was not there, he switched several ignition wires to the wrong sparkplugs.

After I thought I had solved what was a minor problem, I discovered my car ran worse than ever. In fact, it would hardly run at all. I worked long hours before I figured out the wiring problem. I didn't mention to Herb that I knew what had happened.

He had commented once about feeling safer now that I no longer had a key to his house, and I considered this statement a challenge. It influenced my plan of retaliation.

Several weeks went by before an opportunity presented itself. Once again, in October, Herb and his family went to visit his mother-in-law, but this time she was coming back with them to stay for a week.

Gayle had been very concerned about their security ever since the news of robberies in the area. This was at a time when security systems were not common so she had deadbolts installed on the outside doors. These deadbolts turned from the inside and were not keyed on the outside.

The windows in their house were the divided light kind and were secured in place with window putty. I removed this putty, then removed one of the windowpanes, unlocked the window and climbed in. After turning the inside bolts on the outside doors I climbed back out the open window. Closing and locking it, I placed the pane back and applied new putty.

I did not see the family arrive, but over time I was able to piece together the story. They arrived about 2 a.m. and were very tired. In addition, there was some family tension in the car upon arrival. Gayle was stressed, Herb was getting irritated and the mother-in-law was giving too much advice. When they tried to get in the back door the key would not open it. The mother-in-law suggested he was using the wrong key. Gayle asked him if he had bolted the door when they left and had exited through the front door. Herb could not remember but said he would go around to the front door and let them in from the inside. As he walked toward the front, Gayle scolded him to hurry, saying her mother was tired.

After trying the front door several times, he became extremely frustrated, then Gayle appeared – angry. "Herb, what in the world are you doing? Mother is tired. Stop fooling around and open the door."

Herb didn't understand why he could not get into his house. After the long drive, the thinly veiled insinuations from the mother-in-law, the constant nervous corrections from Gayle as she tried to placate that childhood longing to please her mother – he had had it. Animal instinct overruled domestic tranquility.

A neighbor child's tricycle had been left in their yard. It was parked within five feet of where Herb stood listening to his wife castigate him. He reached down, and in a flash – before Gayle could respond – he hurled the tricycle through the living room window. While Gayle stood speechless, he reached in, unlocked the window, opened it and disappeared into the house.

Of course, Herb's little display of temper caused him not only to suffer the condemnation of Gayle, but his mother-in-law made little references from time to time throughout her stay, about – "our Christian duty to control our temper." He also had to suffer the knowing looks and unspoken disapproval that only a mother-in-law can muster.

The next day Gayle herself showed up at my house. In a very strained conversation she elicited a promise from me that I would not engage in any more stupid, inane, childish pranks, even if Herb practiced them on me. This ended our jokes, but not the fun of retelling them over the years. We all remained friends, but when Gayle was around, we did not discuss the jokes.

# CHAPTER 11
## THE CHEESEL

*There is a passion for hunting, something
deeply implanted in the human breast.*

—CHARLES DICKENS

1972: WEST TEXAS, NEAR MEXICAN BORDER — From the accounts I had heard, Dr. Renaldo was brilliant. Ron Davis, my friend, neighbor and fellow airline pilot had told me so on several occasions. He was the oncologist who had treated Ron's wife for breast cancer, and, from all indications, it was in remission. He was highly respected in the medical community, and, although most thought he was a bit of an oddball, his peculiar personality was acceptable, even desirable, for a professional of his intellect.

Ron, several other Delta pilots and I had hunted on a large ranch in far west Texas the previous year. A meeting was arranged at Ron's house to plan the upcoming hunt. Ron had invited Dr. Renaldo to hunt with us, and he was to attend the meeting. Ron had forewarned us that the doctor was very opinionated and could be a bit overbearing.

To say Dr. Renaldo was opinionated was an understatement. He had strong opinions on subjects he knew nothing about. Airline pilots generally have oversized egos, but Dr. Renaldo's ego was as big as Texas. These were dangerous personality traits to bring to our hunt. Some of us felt challenged, indeed, obligated, to at least bring his ego down to the level of our own. It soon became obvious that not only was he an inexperienced hunter, but he had also spent very little time outdoors. He was totally ignorant of the terrain and habitat to which he was committing himself. We considered this lack of knowledge a weakness, and on our hunt, no weakness went unpunished.

Our hunting lease was as wild as any place in the United States. It was 30 miles of dirt road from Ruidosa, Texas, and Ruidosa, a tiny border town, was in the middle of nowhere. Only one person on our hunting ranch spoke English, and, except for a generator, there was no electricity. They raised goats and cattle. Dry and rugged, the mountainous land had little vegetation, mostly wild grass, greasewood, scrub cedar and cactus.

The trip was more than just the chance to bag a desert mule deer. It was about rough living, telling stories, chewing tobacco and spitting in the dirt, drinking whiskey, not bathing and, oh yes, playing practical jokes. Dr. Renaldo knew none of this. He was the perfect target.

On the previous year's hunt, one of the pilots boasted about his ability to tell where and when the deer were moving, and the size of their horns, just by observing and following their tracks. One of our hunters bagged a very large buck, and I got permission to secretly remove its feet. After dark, two of us meticulously made footprints about 50 yards from our camp.

The next morning when the tracks were discovered the expert was called upon to interpret the size and intention of the deer moving in such close proximity to our camp. The tracker proceeded to follow the trail, all the while pontificating about the size of the animal and how the fresh tracks came so close to our campsite. As the hoof prints progressed over a slight rise they led to a pickup truck, which had both doors open. They stopped short of the open door and as the tracker looked up into the truck with a puzzled expression, I exclaimed, "Look here. There are tracks on the other side where he came out of the truck."

Over drinks that night there was a lot of laughing and teasing our tracker as to how a deer opens the door to a pickup truck, what it might have done had the keys been left in the ignition, and what a good job our expert had done.

The ringtail, a common animal found in the area, is about the size of a small raccoon. It looks like a cross between a coon and a house cat. One night, as I slipped my bare feet and legs into my sleeping bag, I felt the unmistakable soft texture of fur and instantly perceived it was moving. I ejected from the bag as if I had been fired from a cannon. My perception was wrong about the movement because the ringtail was not alive, but the effect was the same. There was considerable talk about how much faster I could exit a sleeping bag than I could enter one. Of course, retaliation was in order, but I couldn't decide who the ringtail hunter was.

It was about 700 miles from Houston to our hunting lease. Most hunters drove straight through in one day. Since I was pulling a horse trailer, I stopped in Ozona to spend the night and give my horse a rest. I was the only one who hunted with a horse; the others used four-wheel drive vehicles. Although we didn't know it at the time, the horse was to play a pivotal role during our week in Texas.

Ron, who genuinely wanted the doctor to bag a deer, had arranged for him to be in an ideal hunting spot where a deer was likely to show. A large buck did present himself, but alas, he was gone before the doctor could find him in the scope. Somehow, the doctor managed to turn his blundering into a story that he had intentionally let the buck pass, waiting for a larger buck to appear. Not only was he undeterred by his gaff, he continued to voice his opinion about things he knew nothing about, including flying. You knew it was bad when even Ron grew tired of Dr. Renaldo's arrogance. It was time to take the doctor on a special hunt. It was time for a little humility.

A bobcat hunt was just the way to do it.

Away from the doctor but close enough that we knew he was within earshot, we talked about the bobcats and cougars that roamed the terrain, mentioning several times that there had been sightings of these mean and fearsome creatures. We even got the ranch manager (the only employee who spoke English) to say that he had spotted what he thought was a cougar. We described how the cougar would make a kind of throat clearing, coughing sound, similar to the Mexican jaguar. After I cleared my throat and gave a rendition of this sound, the ranch manager said that it was very similar to what he had heard from the large cat.

As anticipated, Dr. Renaldo became curious and entered into the conversation. It was only then that Ron broached the subject to the doctor of a possible night bobcat hunt. He became very excited about the idea and wanted to do it right away, since he would be leaving the next day.

Out of sight of the doctor, the ranch manager produced an old moth-eaten taxidermied bobcat. It was not a very good likeness in the daytime, but it had glass eyes that would glow realistically at night. In the afternoon, I saddled my horse and, along with the rest of my equipment, attached a sack containing the stuffed bobcat. I informed my fellow hunters I would not be returning until the next afternoon.

My destination was a mesa I had discovered on a previous ride. It was totally inaccessible by vehicle, but the steep, rocky climb was not a problem for my horse. At the eastern edge of the mesa, I could maneuver through some boulders and look down on a ranch road winding around the mountain 100 yards below.

*Me on my horse Ginger*

*Arnie, on our pack*
*Donkey gets the drop on me*

Securing my horse and making camp in the center of the mesa, I walked over to the edge until I could view the road below and placed the stuffed bobcat there. I tied a string to one of its legs and located the other end of the string behind some large rocks where I would be out of sight. Returning to my camp, I cooked supper so the fire could be extinguished before dark.

After dark, I made my way back to the mounted bobcat, positioning myself so I could see the road below. Not long after, truck lights appeared and I watched as the hunting team shined a bright spotlight from the truck up on the mountain above the road. I took my place behind the rocks and picked up the string, waiting for the spotlight to find the stuffed bobcat. When the light picked up the glass eyes, I heard Ron say, "I've got one, now be real quiet and shoot right between the eyes."

"I see it! I see it!" the doctor exclaimed.

When he fired, I jerked the string and the bobcat disappeared. As I pulled it to me in the rocks, an excited Dr. Renaldo yelled, "I got him!"

Then a discussion began between the doctor and Ron about retrieving the dead bobcat. "Suppose he is not dead," I heard the doctor say.

"He's dead. I saw him fall. Go get him. I'll shine the spotlight in front of you."

Reluctantly, Dr. Renaldo began climbing toward the spot where the bobcat had been. When the doctor was close, Ron turned off the spotlight. "KEEP THE LIGHT ON! I CAN'T SEE," the doctor shouted.

At this moment I began my cough imitation of a cougar. "My god," the doctor screamed, "It's not a bobcat – it's a cougar! TURN THE LIGHT ON! TURN THE LIGHT ON!"

I coughed again and Ron pretended he didn't understand what the doctor was saying and yelled up to him, "I'm just going to turn the truck around, I'll be right back."

One more vicious attacking cougar cough and the arrogant, brilliant Dr. Renaldo became a babbling idiot. He half ran and half tumbled off the mountain in the dark. When Ron picked him up, he was incoherent and bleeding from several places.

Dr. Renaldo returned to Houston the next day, but not before he bragged to those who were not on the hunt about how he had shot a cougar.

We stayed several more days and managed to kill two bobcats, which made it possible for us to plan the second part of our ruse with Dr. Renaldo.

The town of Alpine, a hidden jewel that few people ever experience, was a stop on the way to the ranch. It sits on a high plateau with surrounding elevations in excess of 6,000 feet and has some of the most beautiful grassland in the United States. The area is home to large herds of antelope who feed on the grasses.

The antelope is by far the fastest animal in North America. It is so fast that it became a curiosity to scientists interested in evolution. Why are they far faster than they need to be for their survival? The answer is that at one time, long before the first humans set foot on these grassy plains, there were cheetahs, the fastest animal in the world today. And the cheetah on these plains ate antelope. Like the rest of us, Dr. Renaldo had marveled at the speed of the antelope. This gave us the nexus for the scientific leg of our hoax.

Our plan was to use both bobcats to make one rogue taxidermy. We would cut one in two just behind the front legs and cut the other just in front of the back legs. When the long pieces were joined the appearance was a cat-like animal with a body about three feet long. This animal would have a cat face and legs, but because of the long body it would also resemble a very large weasel. We planned to present him with his elongated stuffed trophy so he could show it off in his office and brag about it to his staff and patients.

Now for the story on just exactly what Dr. Renaldo had bravely faced that frightful night while on adventure in west Texas: during the pre-historic period when cheetahs roamed the west Texas plains, there was a very large weasel, which also preyed on the giant jackrabbits in the area. Somehow, instead of becoming extinct, the cheetah and the weasel merged through crossbreeding.

We were prepared to furnish the doctor with copies of museum literature describing the ancient existence of both the cheetah and the weasel. Along with real copies from the museum authenticating the west Texas weasel and cheetah, we would present false documents proving the very unlikely, but nevertheless, real example of crossbreeding between the species resulting in the existence of the *"cheesel."*

What Dr. Renaldo thought was a bobcat turned into what he later thought was a cougar, but it was neither. What he shot was a rarely seen west Texas cheesel.

This was our plan but, unfortunately, it was not to be. Ron got cold feet. He was afraid that if the doctor found out the truth, his ego would be damaged to the point that it could affect the treatment of Ron's wife. Dr. Renaldo was presented a real stuffed bobcat, and to this day he is probably telling his brave story.

Oh, one more detail: when he shot at the stuffed bobcat, he missed.

# CHAPTER 12
## BIG MAMMA AND THE CHICKEN MAN

*If you do a job too well,*
*you'll get stuck with it.*

—UNKNOWN

1976: CONROE, TEXAS — Scott stormed breathlessly into the house screaming, "Cindy, Cindy, come quick – she's having babies – Big Mamma, she's having babies. I saw one already born, running around."

I was out of town flying a trip for Delta, my wife was at the store and our four children were at the farm. Cindy, the eldest at 13, and the family expert on all things animal, was expected to know what to do. All four children made a dash to the barn. Sure enough, there was Big Mamma lying on her side, grunting as piglet number two started to emerge. Cindy quickly crawled into the straw-covered pen and began her porcine midwife apprenticeship.

While Cindy was cleaning the birth sac away from the second pig, she instructed the other children to catch the first born and offer it one of Big Mamma's 12 teats. Thus, a loose assembly line was formed and continued until the 10th and last pig was attached to a teat and ingesting its first warm milk. When I returned the children proudly showed off the pigs as if they had created them. All 10 pigs lived and thrived, thanks to their critical early care.

In 1975, I moved my family 40 miles north of Houston to our newly purchased farm outside of Conroe, Texas. Like many restless young men, I wanted to recreate for them my idyllic youth. But I had a problem: a great deal of our satisfaction with this experiment depended on acceptance by the local agricultural community. Didn't matter that I grew up on a farm. I could tell where I stood, *a farming airline pilot? Come on, what could he know of cows and pigs or growing hay? He probably couldn't even grow chickens.*

That first year while I grew hay, I started introducing my children to the world of animal husbandry.

My son, Scott, age 11, raised Wilbur, a hog named after the charismatic pig in *Charlotte's Web*. Wilbur became a pet. He weighed 300 pounds when we took him to the qualifying weigh-in for the show at the county fair. The upper weight limit was 260, so we ate Wilbur. I had taught the children that farm animals were all about consumption. I grossly underestimated their sensitivity. Serving up Wilbur was a mistake; Scott would not even look at a one of his pork chops.

With Scott you never knew what he was thinking. You just knew he always had something on his mind. When he was about six years old, I had a cigar smoking habit. Once during supper I asked all the children if they could be anything in the world, what would it be. After listening to all the fantastic imaginings from the other children, it was Scott's turn. He simply stated, "I'd smoke the cigars and give the orders."

Scott's twin brother, Brad, nursed a very young bottle-fed calf we called Moo Cow. She did not meet the same fate as Wilbur. Instead, we bred her and she birthed many calves. When she was young she would stand outside the house bawling for Brad to bring her milk bottle. She followed not only the children around the yard, but also Wilbur. She and Wilbur never quite figured out what species they were, but whatever it was, they thought they were the same.

As for Brad, in addition to being good with baby cows, he also liked playing with fire and building homemade bombs. Once I came home from flying and discovered my entire hay field had been burned.

Cindy had a barrel racing quarter horse and raised chickens, opossums, snakes, honeybees and any other living creature that she could take in. When guests arrived, her favorite thing was to show up with her five-foot pet boa constrictor wrapped around her neck.

Rebecca was seven and pretended to raise everything, but mostly stood in awe at the chaos and wonder in the lives of her three older siblings.

When Wilbur busted his weigh in, I got the distinct impression we were being laughed at. That, however, was not going to stop us from going and seeing what the fair was all about. A few days before the start, I heard over the radio that KIKR, in conjunction with Montgomery County, would be sponsoring the first official East Texas Piney Woods Hog Calling Contest. This got me to thinking, and that night my family heard some strange hollering at the back of our farm.

I come from a long line of hog callers that goes back more than 100 years to the North Carolina Mountains. The people in those parts had little contact with the more civilized eastern portion of the state. They lived almost entirely from the labor of their own hands, surviving mainly from subsistence farming.

Before blight destroyed three billion chestnut trees along the Appalachian Mountain chain from Maine to Georgia, chestnuts dominated these forests. One of every four trees was a chestnut that commonly grew 100 feet tall. Both man and beast could survive indefinitely in the forest as long as chestnuts were falling.

Smoky Mountain cured hams became famous for a reason. Hams, bacon and shoulders could be kept without refrigeration. Pigs were allowed to roam freely through the forest, eating chestnuts while growing fat for the upcoming winter slaughter, costing the farmer nothing. With his hogs straying a long way from home, hog calling was a necessity. A good caller could project his voice a great distance, reverberating off the mountains, bringing his porkers to the barn. Each caller developed his own cadence and tone for his particular hogs.

My grandfather learned this hog calling from his father, and my father learned it from him and even though our hogs were only in a five-acre wooded lot, my father practiced the call. He also used the same call for the cows. It may have been overkill, but sometimes a man just naturally wants an excuse to holler. And so, I learned the call. I can still hear in my mind his powerful crystal-clear call that I loved to mimic as soon as my voice changed at puberty.

I entered the contest determined to demonstrate that hog calling skills honed under pressure of putting food on the family table were of a quality unknown to the gentleman or hobby farmer. For me, this was a gamble. If I didn't win, I would just be that crazy airline pilot making a fool of himself. But if I won, I would earn some credibility as a farmer. The contestants who preceded me were mostly traditional with a few original. We listened to *piggy, piggy, piggy* and *suwee suwee* and some invented calls that smacked of cute, but would not have turned the head of self-respecting swine.

When it was my turn, I stepped up to the calling line. I imagined my grandfather delivering his clear falsetto that echoed through mountains like a train whistle on a cold winter night. I pictured my hogs on a mountain, just beyond, eating chestnuts. I leaned back and projected my voice not to the crowd, not to the judges – but to the mountain and its bounty of chestnut trees. A hundred years melted away, and I repeated the call that had come down through generations.

The judges' decision was unanimous. I left the fair with the first place trophy and a big-bellied 350-pound sow.

Not long after the prize sow joined our farm, it dawned on me – *that's not just a big belly, she is with pig*! From then on she was known as Big Mamma and settled in to our farm and family as if she'd always known us. Given how great she was with my kids, I figured she might be helpful in my work as a youth leader for the young teens at the Presbyterian Church. On the Sunday afternoons I was in town, they often came to our farm for games.

One of the games I invented was to place two empty buckets 50 feet out from the creek at the back of the farm and give everybody an eight ounce cup. Two teams competed to see who could fill their bucket first. The rules were for each teen to have only one cup and they could not interfere with each other at their buckets or while running with the cup. The kicker here was that there were no rules while in the creek. The game quickly turned to chaos, with everyone ending up soaking wet and muddy from head to toe. The parents were shocked when they came to pick up the kids, but each time we had an event, more teens came.

A game they all loved was the livestock race, which took place in a fenced-in pasture about the size of a football field. The contestants were divided into three teams with each team assigned an animal, either Big Mamma, Moo Cow or a chicken. The game was a race to get an animal from one end of the pasture to the other. No ropes were allowed, and they could not carry the chicken. Otherwise they could try anything they thought would work. Because Moo Cow and Big Mamma were very friendly, the children soon learned that any attempt to scare them toward the finish just caused them to turn toward the agitators so they would pet them. The chicken usually won.

When Big Mamma's piglets grew to about 20 pounds, on teen Sunday I used them for a pig scramble. They were not very tame and were tough to catch. The combination of squealing pigs and squealing children sounded like carnage taking place on the farm.

My standing as a mentor to young livestock growers took a giant leap when I won the Piney Woods Hog Calling contest. The news of my win, along with the winning call, was broadcast over the radio in several counties. People perceived me to be an expert on swine. I became friends with the county agent and had long discussions with farming parents about the upcoming year's projects.

The following year at the fair my children raised several projects for show. Because I knew how to do it and many were too squeamish, our farm became the go-to place for free 4-H pig castrations. One thing I demanded, however, was the young showman had to help. Some got sick, some had tears, but all were proud when it was over.

During those years, while Brad showed steers and Scott showed pigs, Cindy focused on chickens. From her 50 chickens, with Cindy's help, I selected the five best to show. I couldn't tell her, but I never liked chickens. I acquired my distaste as a boy when I had the responsibility of caring for 1,000 without proper equipment. They pecked my barefoot toes. They died in hidden places where I would have to find their smelly, rotting carcasses.

Even the judge of the lowly chickens did not measure up. He was nothing like the lean and cool cattle judge, a professor from Texas A&M who wore a Stetson and ostrich skin cowboy boots and spat tobacco so quick you couldn't tell for sure he was chewing. The chicken judge, although also an expert from A&M, was pudgy and wore a baseball cap. His voice was soft and tentative, as he hitched up his pants. He might have been more at home judging pickles at the home economics show. Besides, it always seemed that most of the chicken exhibitors were girls. But you can't argue with success. Cindy sold a pen of five chickens for $1,000 at the auction, an impressive sum in 1978.

The next year I traveled all over Texas with the county agent picking out show calves and pigs for the county's young livestock growers. Some of these did quite well. And because of Cindy's prize chickens, I was asked by a family for help with their chickens. Even though chickens were not my thing and I wanted to distance myself from them, I still felt a civic responsibility to give a hand.

All baby chickens come in boxes from the hatchery and no selection is possible at that time. Usually 50 are fed out for show and the best five selected from these right before they are to be shown. The family insisted they knew nothing about the attributes of a good show chicken and asked me to select their pen of five. This was a lot of work. All 50 chickens needed to be looked at for the yellowish orange color of fat on the breast, the width and length of breast, the spacing of the bones in the rear, the health of the bird, and even the brightness of the eyes. On top of that, all five had to look alike.

After working half a day, I gave them their five. They won Grand Champion of show, sold the pen for $7,000 and proclaimed me a chicken man. Forget that I had won the hog calling contest, forget that I had castrated the show hogs, and forget that I had a part in selecting many prize large animals. Much to my chagrin, that family gave me all the credit. I was a chicken man.

# ≡ CHAPTER 13 ≡
## THE CRISIS OF KLAUS

*Don't accept your dog's admiration as conclusive evidence that you are wonderful.*

—ANN LANDERS

1976: CONROE, TEXAS — Ted Lockhart was a nice enough captain. He was opinionated and cocksure, but not overbearing. At times, he asserted his opinions of non-flying topics with the aid of his captain's stripes. This tended to irritate me, but he had a good sense of humor, and, for the most part, I enjoyed flying with him.

Ted and I set out on a Boeing 727 to fly a three-day rotation. For all three of those days, I was besieged by his stories of Klaus, the family dog, rescued from the Humane Society.

Ted talked about the large raw-looking rash on the side of Klaus's neck. He said they'd been in and out of the vet's office for the past six months. With no apparent improvement, his veterinary expenses had climbed above $2,000. The bills were causing Ted heartburn, and he had expressed his dissatisfaction to the vet, comparing the vet's attempts to cure Klaus with a pilot's attempts at landing an airplane:

"Damn, Doc, if I took as many attempts at landing an airplane as you have at curing my dog, I'd run out of gas and crash!"

The vet said he, indeed, had run out of gas and still did not know what was wrong with Klaus. He suggested that he might present Klaus as an interesting case study to his alma mater, Texas A&M School of Veterinary Medicine. In the interest of science, the school agreed to do some diagnostic testing on Klaus, so he was transferred there for a week. The college would pay for the diagnostic work; any treatments, however, would have to be paid for by the owner. In his usual salty way, Ted made it clear that he wished he had never heard of the Humane Society or Klaus.

"The dog is just a damn cur. He's been trouble ever since we got him. When we first brought him home, he peed all over the house for a month. I should have taken him back then. Now the son-of-a-bitch has cost me over $2,000, and we still haven't cured the mange on his neck.

"And I don't expect much satisfaction from the high-level observations of a bunch of eggheads at Texas A&M either."

But mange or no mange, vet bills or no vet bills, his wife and children were attached to Klaus.

Returning home from my trip late in the afternoon, I did a few things around the house while listening to my wife expound on the troubles she had had with the children. As usual, she had threatened them with the unknown dire consequences that would happen when their father came home. I listened to the children describe their day, decided the good canceled out the bad, had a couple of beers, and we all ate supper.

After supper, I was in a jocular mood as I began thinking about Ted's dilemma with Klaus and his mounting expenses. Even some very good bird dogs didn't cost as much. Perhaps it was my mood, but an idea popped into my head and long about 8 p.m., I called Ted up.

"Captain Lockhart," I said disguising my voice, "this is Dr. Kruger."

"Yes?"

"I am the veterinarian in charge of the Texas A&M Diagnostic and Research Lab. Your animal was referred to us by Dr. Clark. I apologize for calling so late, but have some information about your dog."

"What is it," Ted asked.

"We did extensive testing on Klaus and have discovered that his kidneys are failing."

"Kidneys! What the hell could this have to do with the mange or whatever he has on his neck?"

"Sir, it doesn't have anything to do with his neck. We discovered the kidney failure during the tests."

"For crying out loud! What is going to happen now?"

"Well, this is the reason I am calling so late. Normally, kidney failure would terminate a pet's life, but in this case you are quite fortunate in that we at the veterinary school have been successful with several canine kidney transplants. By chance, we have a donor match for Klaus that became available today and . . ."

"What! Are you telling me that you want to do a kidney transplant on Klaus, and we still don't even know what is wrong with his neck?"

"This is the reason for my call. It is, of course, your decision."

"Damn! I already have over $2,000 in his neck. How much would this cost?"

"Even though we are very careful with our procedures in these transplants, there are some steps we are able to forego with our canine operations that would reduce the expense over a human transplant."

"How much are we talking about here?"

"Considering that the university would absorb the expense of the observation time, the total would be around $5,000."

"Five thousand dollars! I would then have over $7,000 in vet bills for a cur from the Humane Society – and he would still have the neck problem?"

"That is accurate. We have not solved the problem with his neck as of this time."

"What if we decide not to do the transplant?"

"Klaus will die within a couple of months."

"I need to think about this."

"Of course. Just be aware, however, the donor match for Klaus is time sensitive, and we will need your decision by tomorrow."

"I will talk this over with my vet, and he will be in touch tomorrow."

Keep in mind that in 1976 veterinary transplants were unheard of, and $7,000 was a small fortune.

My wife had heard enough of the conversation to know that I was up to no good. When I explained it to her, she didn't think it was funny; now I was having second thoughts. Maybe Ted actually liked the dog. Maybe his sense of humor wasn't what I thought it was. Maybe it was the same as my wife's. I pondered the situation and decided to call my friend Dick Fulmer (another crazy airline pilot) and tell him the story. He laughed and suggested I let Ted suffer the full consequences of the joke. I felt better as I hung up.

Shortly after, I got a call from Dick's wife, Bobbie, who was friends with Ted's wife and had been on the phone with her. Bobbie had overruled Dick and was upset, insisting that I immediately call Ted and tell him the truth. She told me Ted's whole family was distressed because he was considering allowing Klaus to expire. It seems Ted's wife had said some very critical things about her unfeeling, callous husband, and I was going to ultimately be blamed for a marriage crisis.

*My God, I didn't want this. Things were spinning out of control.*

I called Ted and confessed. He did not laugh. Instead, he relayed to me the trouble I had caused by not calling sooner to tell him it was a joke. First, he *had* called his vet and told him about his conversation with the fictitious Dr. Kruger. He had chewed out Dr. Clark because he did not know about the kidney transplant. His vet then called the head of The School of Veterinary Medicine who said he did not know Dr. Kruger, but would find him and report back. According to Ted, a chain reaction had been set off at Texas A&M, which would be hard to clear up. Phone calls were bouncing around through the school bureaucracy. This was all in progress when I called.

On top of this, Ted informed me that he had been getting so much heat from his wife and kids about not proceeding with the transplant that he had already called his vet back and said he had decided to go through with the transplant. Now, probably as we were speaking, Ted's veterinarian was on the phone telling Texas A&M to inform Dr. Kruger the transplant was a go.

And in Ted's own words, "And now, Goddamn you, Taylor, I have to call back my vet, and tell him to cancel the operation and quit looking for Dr. Kruger because he is you."

Even though I had overestimated Ted's sense of humor, I was sure he was in possession of a large ego, and he would not like being snookered. He might get even, but the story would not be told unless I told it. I was cautious about telling it for years – and I never did find out if Klaus's rash went away.

# CHAPTER 14
## NO EXCUSE, SIR

*Good judgment comes from experience
and experience comes from bad judgment.*

—RITA MAE BROWN

1980: JACKSON, MISSISSIPPI — My state of mind was bad. Divorce after 18 years of marriage, custody of four teenagers, flying my Delta trips, juggling schedules, fixing family crises at home – all of that was stressful enough. But then I added girlfriend problems. The tag that I had been quick to attach to others now belonged to me – I was crazy.

After landing the Boeing 727 in Jackson, Mississippi, we began a 16-hour layover. I was dreading the layover. I had a girlfriend in Jackson and had made up my mind to break off the relationship. I thought I was in love with Lisa back in Houston. My troubled psyche had arrived at a desired conclusion, and now I was backing in the facts to support it. Lisa was perfect in every way – or so I thought.

The layover did not go well. The following morning, I arrived at the airport, haggard and depressed. My co-pilot was both proficient and perceptive. He asked on two occasions if I was all right. I assured him I was, but I thought I detected him looking at me in a concerned way. Of course, this irritated me.

On taxi out we were informed that one of the cross-connecting taxiways was closed for construction. To get to the departure runway we would need to take the reverse high-speed connector. A high-speed connector is positioned at a 45-degree angle to the taxiway so that it can be taken without slowing. A reverse high speed requires a 135-degree turn. It needs to be negotiated slowly with caution.

It had rained throughout my troubled layover, and Jackson had accumulated almost two inches by our departure time the next morning. I had trouble concentrating on the taxi out to the runway. *Had I done the right thing? I gave up a good woman for one I wasn't even sure would love me.* I had envisioned doing the right thing – the courageous thing. Now that I had broken her heart I wasn't sure – *was I just being stupid? God, if I am in love, why am I miserable?*

Without proper consideration, I took the turn on the reverse high speed. I cut the corner. The left main gear rolled off the concrete and sank sickly into the mud. I tried once to power it out – hopeless.

The airplane wing slumped toward the mud. By now, many of my passengers realized what had happened. I had seen an airplane stuck before. The comments, including my own, were not kind toward the captain. Humiliation overwhelmed me. The co-pilot and engineer looked at me to see what would be my next move. My co-pilot had already indicated his concern. To his credit he said nothing.

For a few seconds, I lowered my head and closed my eyes. I could feel my command authority slipping away. My mind flashed back to those trying days as a plebe at The Citadel. *No excuse, sir. No excuse.* Whatever was wrong, no excuse was all we were allowed to say. This was drilled into our heads so as to last a lifetime. A commander takes responsibility – there is no excuse.

I picked up the phone and punched the passenger address button. "Ladies and gentlemen, this is your captain speaking. I have made a most embarrassing error. I have taxied your airplane into the mud. I want you to understand that this is entirely my fault. There is no danger, but it will result in a flight delay. Please be patient while we contact maintenance to help assess our situation. As soon as I have more information, I will be back in touch."

I hung up the phone and told the co-pilot to contact the tower and let them know we would be blocking the taxiway. I contacted Jackson maintenance. When maintenance arrived, they were cordial and business-like, but I could imagine the comments later: *So this is why they make the big bucks.* Mechanics are hired for their expert skills and these do not necessarily include people skills. I braced myself for the biting comments.

Maintenance determined digging and ground matting would be required. They requested we offload the passengers to reduce weight.

Next, I told the Jackson station manager of our dilemma and the need for a bus. I also implored him to provide the passengers with any comforts he could. He authorized food to be served in the terminal.

Another difficult announcement – I informed my passengers they would need to be bused back to the terminal and that their delay would be extensive.

I then told the engineer to ask the lead flight attendant to come to the cockpit. Luckily for me, she was a good one – attractive, good humored, but best of all, perceptive about the needs of anxious passengers. I apologized for what had happened and asked her to help me. Would she see to it that everything possible was done to appease the passengers? (I found out later she and the other flight attendants stayed with the passengers and served their needs, even while they were in the terminal.)

When the bus arrived, I made the announcement that we would offload through the front cabin door, and I would be present for any questions. I stood in the cockpit door and looked at every passenger, giving each a chance to complain. No one did.

While maintenance was at work, I got a call from the chief pilot in Dallas. He was a friend, and Jackson fell under his jurisdiction. He said he was available if any assistance was needed. This was as far as the incident went. I heard nothing further from any Delta people other than my crew.

After working in the mud for an hour, the expert Delta mechanics powered our sturdy 727 back to the concrete. We returned to the gate to re-board the passengers. Once again, I greeted each passenger and was surprised to hear no complaints.

Upon landing in Atlanta, I made another announcement. "Ladies and gentlemen, I want to thank all of you for your kind patience throughout this trying flight. If any of you would like to express your dissatisfaction, I will be in the doorway to the cockpit. Please do not blame other Delta people. If you would like to complain to someone else, I will provide you with my business card."

To my surprise, as they disembarked, I received smiles and praise, but not one complaint. One passenger stopped long enough to tell me it was refreshing in today's world for someone to accept responsibility.

After unloading about half the people, there was a gap in the departure line. An attractive young woman was holding up the line while she and her male friend gathered their bags. As she looked up and saw me, she ran forward. To the surprise of everyone, she threw her arms around my neck and started thanking me over and over – tears in her eyes – smiling, laughing – genuinely grateful. We all were baffled. She turned to her young seatmate who had come forward, shouting, "He did it! He did it! He finally asked me to marry him! You made it happen – it was fate – the mud, the delay, the stress. He proposed. Oh, thank you! Thank you!"

The co-pilot's prior concern about my mental state had given way to compliments on a job well done. "It's easy to command a good situation," he said. "I have learned something about how to take command of a bad situation." That same year, he became a Delta captain.

I was a better captain after that. I had more confidence in my command ability. During the entire episode, I had not thought about the other stresses in my life. From then on I left my other life behind when I put on my captain's hat and headed for the airport. I became relaxed and stress free when on the job – the greatest job in the world.

None of my old girlfriends worked out. I had to move to Atlanta to find the right woman who would become my second wife. By then I wasn't crazy, a little strange maybe – but not crazy.

But I get ahead of myself. The following story is the conclusion of the saga with Lisa, the cause of my angst and, not withstanding "no excuse, sir," the reason I had taxied into the mud.

# CHAPTER 15

## IRS RED SPOTS

*We'll try to cooperate fully with the IRS,*
*because as citizens, we feel*
*a strong patriotic duty not to go to jail.*

—DAVE BARRY

1980: HOUSTON, TEXAS — Lisa was beautiful, sophisticated and smart – I was smitten. She could be soft and sweet, and I needed that. We talked constantly, exposing secrets, confessing failures, acknowledging needs, and, after dating five months, we pledged our love for one another. I was euphoric. Everything was right again. My problems disappeared, and I loved the world.

But every now and then I had a glimpse of another side of Lisa, a side that I dared not explore or even acknowledge to myself. She was deeply bitter about her ex-husband, at times exhibiting irrational anger and a burning, seemingly insatiable desire to get even. During these moments, I felt a sense of foreboding, like something was lurking just outside the door. I tried to rationalize that this was not my problem – but it was. Occasionally, she seemed to confuse me with her ex. At other times, I was vehemently warned to never be anything like him.

The day after Lisa and I had confessed our love for each other, I departed on a two-day trip in an ecstatic mood. I returned home tired, but eager to talk to Lisa. Before I could call, she called me. "Steve," she said. "I have been thinking. I was wrong – I don't love you. I think it would be best if we ended our relationship."

If she'd hit me with a sledgehammer, I couldn't have felt worse. I didn't understand. I told her so. But she would not give me an explanation. I was devastated. At 44, I had lived long enough to know meanness. I had encountered mean boys growing up and some mean-spirited adults. I had seen the ugliness of war. But until meanness is cloaked in the sweet tender bosom of one you have loved, you don't know meanness.

Whether consciously or subconsciously, Lisa needed to hurt somebody, and I was it. She was seeing a psychiatrist to deal with the bitter pain of divorce from an unfaithful spouse. My stress level was high in the aftermath of my own divorce compounded by having custody of four teenagers. Plus I was lonely. We saw salvation in each other, but I refused to see the caution signs that were there. I took the bait, and now I was thrashing in a love trap.

We were broken up, but I kept finding excuses to see her, desperate to understand. At times she was nice, and I would find myself lulled into hopefulness that we might get back together. But then, out of the blue, she would pierce my heart again. She had heard about some of my practical jokes, but insisted that since she hadn't witnessed any jokes, she doubted they were true. The very fact that she had not been a party to one of my pranks should have been a warning that I was acting out of character. The truth was that I had put her on a pedestal and did not want to see her suffer through the embarrassment of a good hoax. Instead of seeing my concern for her, she saw self-serving dishonesty.

I did eventually cease communication, not because I felt closure, but because I could no longer stand my own humiliation.

About four months after Lisa and I quit speaking, I received a letter from the IRS about an item on my tax return. I was reminded of Lisa and thought about how I had helped her with her taxes. Even though my pain had subsided, I still felt she deserved retribution, if not for heartbreak, then for the girlfriend I gave up for her and for steering the plane off the taxiway in Jackson.

A plan began to hatch.

The next day I ran into my friend, Bob Norris, in the Delta pilot lounge. As usual he had a story:

He and his crew were on a layover having drinks in his room. The door was partially open, and as they relaxed, Bob began to focus on a loud conversation between two lawyers in the room across the hall. The louder voice was Rudy's, and he was bragging about a girl named Carla he had just met in the lounge.

"Man, that Carla-something-or-other was hot," Rudy said. "She was starting to come on to me until that other girl, what's-her-face, said they had to go."

"Come on, Rudy," the other lawyer said, "they're married."

"So are you – so am I. Who gives a flip? We're 2,000 miles from home."

The wheels of Bob's trickster brain began to spin. He took one of the flight attendants aside and explained his plan. After a quick rehearsal, the flight attendant called Rudy's room.

"Rudy, this is Carla, remember me? We met in the lounge."

"Oh yeah, of course I remember. I was sorry you had to leave."

"Well, I left because of my friend, but she's gone now, and I was wondering if I could come up for a drink."

"Sure . . . yeah. Come on up."

When Rudy hung up, he flew into a frenzy to get dressed, opening drawers and closet doors, and ordering his friend to leave. "I told you she liked me. Come on, man, you gotta go!"

"All right, all right, I'm leaving, but how will I know when I can come back?"

"I will crack the door open when you can come back in. If the door is closed, go away."

The roommate left. A half hour later, Bob called Rudy.

"Yes," Rudy said.

"Lemme speak ta Rudy," Bob said, adopting a thick Jersey accent.

"This is he."

"Rudy, dis is Angelo Costantini. You messin' wid my wife?"

"I . . . I don't know what you're talking about."

"If Carla's wid ya, you're a dead man. If she ain't, I'm thinkin' 'bout whackin' you anyhow."

"Carla's not here – ah, I don't know who Carla is . . . you've got the wrong number."

"I got your number, buddy – doen shit me."

Bob hung up and all was quiet across the hall.

The next morning Bob was in the hotel lobby early. At the desk, he asked to see the hotel roster claiming he wanted to call a crew member. Next to Rudy's room number was his Houston home address and phone number. It happened that Bob and his crew would be returning to Houston late that very afternoon. In the Houston crew lounge, Bob called Rudy's home. A woman, presumably his wife, answered. Bob asked to speak to Rudy, but the woman said Rudy was not home. She offered to take a message.

"Jus' tell him dat Angelo Costantini called. I'm in town an' I'd like to see him."

Even before Bob had finished his story, I was fleshing out my plan. Bob was the best con man, straight man and hoaxer on Delta Air

Lines. He was just the guy to help me pull it off.

Income taxes were the key to the hoax. At tax time, I had convinced Lisa that she did not need an accountant. I coached her through, applying my knowledge of the process from years of doing my own taxes. There were some complications, though. It was the first return since her divorce, and her ex was involved in a business that made a lot of money. Several times Lisa had told me that he would go ballistic if the IRS were to question him, and she was concerned that her deductions might trigger an audit. She wanted to know what would happen if she were audited. I explained that she should not fear an audit so much that she cheated herself, that as long as she had a good argument and documentation, the worst that could happen was the deduction would be disallowed. Still, she was anxious about this and wanted to know in detail what might happen. I told her that it could range from anything from a few questions to a full-blown audit where every line on the return would be examined. That was a general audit, I told her, reassuring her they were very rare.

So now, ten months later, with the help of Bob Norris, it was time for Lisa to get a call from the IRS.

"May I speak to Ms. Lisa Talbert please?"

"To whom am I speaking?"

"This is Nathan Hall representing the taxpayer compliance division of the Internal Revenue Service. Is this Ms. Talbert?"

"Yes."

"Ms. Talbert, I have before me your 1980 tax return. I have a few questions that probably can be cleared up over the phone, but first I would like remind you that we at the IRS are government servants and we work for you, the American taxpayer."

Lisa was quiet.

"Now, Ms. Talbert, I notice on your 1040A you have deducted a considerable sum for personal sales taxes. Do you have receipts for all of these deductions?"

"I can show receipts for some, but some I had to calculate based on the money spent. I . . . I thought . . . "

"Ms. Talbert we here at treasury sometimes provide a certain leeway in our code, but waiving documentation is not allowed. Is it my understanding that you do not have receipts for all the deductions you claimed?"

"Well . . . I do have . . . ah . . ."

"Let's move to your interest deduction. I noticed that along with mortgage interest you also deducted points paid on a loan. Are you aware that the stated points are not necessarily all deductible?"

"It is what was shown on . . . ah . . . the . . ."

"Ms. Talbert, did your ex-husband deduct any of this interest on his return?"

"I don't know. He doesn't share his finances with me."

"But he does share his income. Is that not correct?"

"Well, I do get some money . . . but . . ."

"Ms. Talbert, is it not true that your ex-husband has a very high income, and that your divorce arrangement shares some of this?"

"I . . . eally can't discuss his finances."

"Of course, I apologize. The reason I asked the question was that there is the possibility that with commingled income and the crossover of divorce settlement there can be some duplicate deductions and misrepresented income. I am going to recommend a complete audit of his taxes going back at least one extra year so we will have more concrete information."

"You're going to audit my ex-husband?"

"Yes, from the evidence I hear today, I believe this case should be greatly expanded. Ms. Talbert, are you familiar with the term *general audit?*"

"I think so . . . it . . . "

"We must end this conversation for now. I have a considerable amount of paperwork to write up. I will be back in touch in a few days. In the meantime, you should gather all evidence you have in preparation for a *general audit.* Thank you for your time. Good day."

Although I had not talked to Lisa in months, I got an icy call from her minutes after Bob hung up.

"Steve, you have really messed me up. I got a call from the IRS, and they are questioning the very things you told me were okay."

"Listen, Lisa, remember I told you not to go ballistic about an audit. The worst they can do is disallow the deduction in question."

"Dammit, Steve, you are so wrong. They are going to audit my ex, and believe me, he will make my life miserable."

"I told you before, you can probably clear up the items in question and they will back off. The only thing you have to worry about is a *general audit.*"

I heard a quaver in her voice and thought she might cry. Had she, I would have softened and told her it was a joke. But Lisa was proud; she rose to the occasion. She became very belligerent.

"Listen, you son-of-a-bitch, they are giving me a *general audit* and it's your fault."

"Lisa, I know this is going to be a nightmare. If I could help, I would, but this is beyond my ability. I recommend you contact a good tax attorney."

Bob and I had some good laughs and decided to give it one day before owning up. In the meantime I gave Bob some more information on Lisa. Once when we were dating, I was admiring her in her bikini when I noticed some small red dots on her belly. I asked her if they were insect bites. Lisa was upset I had noticed them. She told me she had mentioned the spots to her doctor, and he said they were the first signs of age spots. I could tell she was sensitive about them and so I was careful not to mention them again.

After giving Lisa a full day to stress out and fight with her ex, Bob called.

"Ms. Talbert, this is Nathan Hall, your IRS case manager. How are you today?"

"Considering the circumstances, I have been better."

"Are you referring to your upcoming audit?"

"Yes."

"I became aware of some information that will necessitate a change in your situation. Your audit has been cancelled."

"I don't understand, could . . . could you elaborate?"

"We here at Internal Revenue Service have certain ethics we must adhere to in relation to our clients, and it has come to our attention that you have a certain physical condition that would fall under these ethics rules."

"I . . . I don't understand."

"Ms. Talbert, we do not audit women with little red dots on their belly."

She was silent, but not for long – "*That bastard!*"

# CHAPTER 16
## CAPTAIN FRENCH BREAD

*The only difference between me
and a madman is I'm not mad.*

—SALVADOR DALI

1983: PHILADELPHIA, PENNSYLVANIA — As we leveled at 33,000 feet, I noticed a bright light in front of the airplane. I discussed it with air traffic controllers, and we determined that it was a large weather balloon 50 miles away at an altitude of more than 10 miles. The sun had set about an hour earlier, so at our altitude it was dark. The balloon, though, was still in daylight and shone much like the moon.

Co-pilot Rick Moore and I had departed Atlanta for Philadelphia with a good group of flight attendants we knew from a previous trip.

I grinned at Rick and rang the call button. When Lynn, the first class flight attendant appeared, I confided, "Listen, I don't want you to be alarmed, but I think you need to know we might have to take some evasive action."

She was alarmed, of course, and responded, "What's wrong?"

"Well, nothing at the moment, but if you look out the windshield you will see something that looks like some kind of UFO or flying saucer. It has been tracking us for the last half hour." Lynn's eyes themselves grew as big as saucers.

"I see it, I see it. What's it doing?"

"It just came from out of nowhere and appeared off to the right, real close, and then it zipped to the other side. At one point, it hovered right over the cockpit and was so bright I couldn't look at it. We're doing about 500 knots, and it is now exactly matching our speed."

It should be noted that it did, indeed, appear to be matching our speed. Because of its great distance, the change in our relative positions was imperceptible.

Lynn gasped and left the cockpit, soon returning with flight attendant Sue Ellen, who seemed more excited about the news of seeing a flying saucer than worried about our flight. They were instructed, above all, to be calm and not upset the passengers. We would be in touch if necessary.

On landing, we discovered our hoax had backfired. Contrary to my instructions, Sue Ellen had told some passengers in coach, and they planned to contact the news media. It took some doing for me to convince them that what the attendant had seen from the cockpit was nothing more than a weather balloon.

We had a 24-hour layover in downtown Philadelphia at the famous Bellevue-Stratford Hotel, where I had been assigned a spacious room. The crew was invited to bring their liquor and come to my room for a debriefing.

In those days it was common for crewmembers to carry some type of spirits in their bag, there being no TSA, no locked doors, and no metal detectors. The FAA had a rule of no drinking within eight hours of flying; however, the company rule was no drinking within 24 hours of flying. The FAA rule was followed, but the company rule usually was not. The general understanding was that the company rule had been created to enable them to hang a crewmember out to dry if he embarrassed the airline with inappropriate behavior, and drinking was involved. The message was drink if you will, but keep a low profile.

After some teasing about the flying saucer and a couple of rounds of libations and laughing, we received a knock on the door. It was hotel security asking us to keep it quiet, because there had been a complaint.

Keeping in mind the low profile rule, we quieted down. Shortly after, Lynn excused herself to use the bathroom. Although a grand hotel, the Bellevue-Stratford was very old. The doors and windows were large and heavy, with many coats of paint. The solid wood bathroom door would not shut completely, which Lynn found unsatisfactory. She complained that she did not trust the rest of us with the door cracked open, and she continued to slam and pull at it. I stood up and did a linebacker ram on the door with my shoulder. It closed and latched.

After she completed her business, Lynn tried to open the door, but it wouldn't budge. Turns out Lynn was not only shy about bathrooms, she was claustrophobic. Her distress mounted rapidly until she was sobbing and beating the door with her fists. Both Rick and I pulling together could not open it. Aware of the noise this was generating, I implored Lynn to calm down, reassuring her we would get her out. But my efforts did nothing to quiet her. Meanwhile, Rick had disappeared. When he reappeared he was carrying a flat 16-inch pry bar. I learned later that he carried this in his suitcase. It was not unusual for crewmembers to carry strange equipment with them.

We went to work on the door and had it open in short order. Just then, there was another knock. I answered, fearing another visit from security. This time it was the hotel manager. The scene he encountered as he stepped into the room was, a red-faced and tear-stained woman, a couple of whiskey bottles and a man with a pry bar in hand, next to a damaged door.

"You were warned about the noise," the manager said. "You are destroying hotel property, and who knows what else is going on. I will be contacting Delta Air Lines about this."

This was bad. This was very, very bad. The situation was my responsibility, but all of us would suffer. I had to do something quick.

"Sir," I said with a calm and authoritative voice. "I understand your concern, and I know this looks suspicious, but before you leap to conclusions you need to be aware that your hotel has serious safety issues. The Airline Pilots Association and Delta Air Lines are very concerned about hotel safety. I also know that the Philadelphia fire department always wants to be aware of fire code violations. This door that we had to pry open was so stuck that if there had been a fire, this young lady could have perished. I am sure you have many other doors with similar problems. I will be informing all of these authorities about this deficiency."

The hotel manager paused as he absorbed the comment. "If you don't say anything," he said, "this incident is concluded."

Our party broke up, and we went to bed. On our second day we were scheduled to fly from Philadelphia to New Orleans and then to Cleveland. We would layover with the same flight attendants in Cleveland. I was a little subdued because of our close call the previous night, but apparently Lynn was not.

Thirty minutes before descent into New Orleans, Rick left the cockpit and was gone longer than normal. When he returned, he had a mischievous look in his eye. I knew something was up, so I tried to wheedle it out of him. Finally, he told me that Lynn was determined to get even with me about the flying saucer and bathroom incidents. She apparently blamed me for jamming the door that exposed her phobia.

After some coaxing, Rick told me about their plan: when we checked into the hotel in Cleveland, the flight attendants would suggest that we all meet in the hotel bar. After everyone had gone to their respective rooms, Rick would return to the front desk, give them my room number and tell them he was having trouble with his key. If he could secure a key to my room, he would give it to Lynn. This key swap was easier than it might seem because airline crews usually had their own room roster and often signed themselves in.

Lynn would wait long enough to be sure I had left for the bar and would then enter my room and steal my uniform pants. This would have been a troublesome situation had she accomplished it. I would not have missed the uniform until I was dressing for our morning pick up, which would not have given me much time to decide what to do. I would have had to put on civilian clothes, knowing everyone would deny they had anything to do with the missing pants. This was a good prank that deserved an appropriate response.

In the New Orleans airport terminal was a French bread shop. I sometimes picked up a baguette if New Orleans was my last stop before returning home. In addition to regular size baguettes, they also carried a smaller size. My interest was in the small baguette. These delicious baguettes were each hand-fashioned, which meant they varied in size and shape. I went to the bin containing the small baguettes and inspected several until I found what I was looking for. It was 12 inches long and two inches in diameter with a slight bulge at the end.

The flight to Cleveland was scheduled to last about an hour

and 45 minutes. When we leveled off at cruise altitude, I called Sue Ellen on the phone in coach. I explained that I wanted to make some red marks to identify some important points on my approach plates and asked her if she had any red fingernail polish. She did and brought it to me. After she departed the cockpit, I took out my French bread and carefully painted the bulge at the end with the fingernail polish and returned it to the bread bag.

While checking into the hotel in Cleveland, right on cue, Lynn suggested we meet at the bar in 30 minutes. We all agreed and went to our rooms to change into civilian clothes.

Using shoe laces, I attached the bread to a pair of shorts and then put them on. I added another pair of shorts over this and passed the bread through the fly. It was impressive. When I moved, it swung from side to side. I went into the bathroom and stood in the tub behind the shower curtain and waited.

Soon, I heard Lynn working the key to my door. Looking around the shower curtain, I could see her searching for my pants, which hung in the small closet next to the bathroom. When she opened the closet door and pulled out my pants, I came bounding out of the bathroom with a growl – the bread swinging. Lynn looked down at the red-tipped baguette, a metronome oscillating from side to side. Wide-eyed and horrified, she squealed, dropped my pants and fled the room.

The next morning, the flight attendants departed on a different flight, and I did not see them again for some time, but word got back to me that there was a young Chicago captain known as *Captain French Bread.*

# ≡ CHAPTER 17 ≡
## CUT 'N SHOOT

*"All new states are invested, more or less, by a
class of noisy, second-rate men who are
always in favor of rash and extreme measures,
but Texas was absolutely overrun by such men."*

—SAM HOUSTON

1985: CONROE, TEXAS — Quincy Fowler was a violent man. At least he had a violent reputation, and he seemed to cherish that reputation. His foul-mouthed wife told him she was leaving and wanted a divorce. He made it known that anybody assisting her in this endeavor would incur the full measure of his wrath.

Sometime during the divorce proceedings, a courier arrived with papers for Quincy. The house, which had never been painted, was landscaped with a dirt yard and several old pieces of machinery. Quincy sat on his front porch wearing overalls and no shirt, his ample belly spilling over the sides of the bib. Chickens pecked around the front steps as the courier asked if he was Mr. Fowler. Quincy spat a stream of tobacco juice, glared menacingly at the messenger and took the delivery. As he looked at the information, one of his chickens jumped up on the end of the porch. Without getting out of his chair, Quincy retrieved his 12-gage shotgun from inside the front door. Given the closeness of the wall and ceiling, the blast was deafening. Chicken blood and feathers exploded all over one end of the porch and dirt yard.

"I told them chickens not to get on my porch," Quincy said.

The terrified courier left. Quicker than you could say Quincy Fowler, word spread around the Montgomery County legal community, and Mrs. Fowler could not find a lawyer to represent her in her divorce.

Cut 'N Shoot, Texas, is a small town in Montgomery County, about six miles outside of Conroe. It did not get its name from cutting cattle and driving them into a chute. The name was actually derived in 1912, when a confrontation between two church factions frightened a small boy. Evidently, to escape the conflict, he said he would cut around the corner and shoot through the bushes. During the East Texas oil boom of the 20s and 30s, the mixture of oilfield roughnecks and cowboys did provoke some cutting and shooting. Through the years the more violent meaning of the name endured. Quincy Fowler lived in Cut 'N Shoot.

Two miles on the other side of Conroe, I owned a small farm. I was divorced and struggling to raise four teenage children while flying for Delta Airlines. I did not like the East Texas rednecks. The previous year I had packed one of my sons off to a New Hampshire prep school, and part of the reason was to expose him to cultures far removed from this redneck world. But there were some aspects that agreed with me. I craved the simpler times where problems were solved not through litigation, but person to person. It appealed to me that, in Texas, one was less likely to flip the bird at a fellow driver, because the other driver might want to fight, and that fight might get deadly.

I had practiced this type of conflict resolution when a controversy developed over my hayfield. On my farm, I was growing a crop of highly fertilized hay that promised to bring top dollar. Through this hay field was a wide easement for a high-tension power line. Every few years, the power company bush-hogged their right-of-ways to keep the access open and the brush from growing too high. There was no reason to mow on my farm, however, since I kept the easement in excellent condition.

One afternoon while the mowing machines were on someone else's property, I talked to the driver to make sure he understood not to mow my hay. He said he had been instructed to mow everything. Since he seemed insistent, I called the power company office, and they agreed not to mow it.

After returning from a Delta trip late one afternoon, I was incensed to discover part of my hayfield within the right-of-way had been mowed. Two large tractors were on the edge of my property where they had been left at the end of the day's mowing.

When the operator returned to work the next morning neither tractor would start. After working on them for several hours, the operator gave up, and a large truck arrived to haul the tractors to the shop. They never returned to my property. They got the message, Texas style.

A habit of East Texas rednecks, which enraged me, had to do with their garbage and trash. Many lived in places that did not have garbage service, or some just did not want to pay for service. Instead of traveling to an approved disposal spot, they threw it along the side of the road.

My farm had about 1,000 feet along a road leading to a scattering of low-rent houses. My most infuriating regular chore was walking along this section of road picking up the trash some low-life had thrown along my fence. Then the day came when someone actually sped by while I was fuming over the chore and threw a bag of garbage at my feet.

It was in this state that I observed an open-bed one-ton truck filled with trash pulling into the vacant property next door. The driver got out and proceeded to offload his trash in plain view of my house. I rushed across my pasture before he could get away.

"What in the hell do you think you're doing?"

To my surprise he did not look guilty or cowed.

"Dumpin' garbage," he said.

I was far from mollified.

"Let me tell you something," I said, looking him squarely in the eye. "I am going back to my house to get my shotgun, and if you are here when I get back, I will blow out the tires on your truck."

Returning to the house in a rage, I retrieved a shotgun and loaded several shells on my way back out the door. To my amazement, he had resumed unloading the trash. He stopped working when he saw me and got down from the truck. I fired three shots at one side, hitting the dual wheels on the back and the front tire. The man climbed into the cab and sped away on three flat tires, and I went home to cool off.

My younger daughter, and the only one of my children still attending the local school, would not be home until mid afternoon. The first thought I had as my rational mind returned was, *God, I don't want my children to know about this.* As I went through events in my mind, I told myself I had accomplished what I set out to do . . . but something didn't seem right. *Why was he so smug?*

A couple hours after the incident, a police car drove into my yard and an officer got out, surveying the property. I walked outside and greeted him before he got to the door. After confirming my identity, he said, "Mr. Taylor, I have here a warrant for your arrest for attempted murder."

I was taken aback. Neither of us spoke for a few seconds. He seemed not to be afraid or in a hurry. I needed to think – *what could I say to slow this down?*

The officer had said he had a warrant, but he had not said I was under arrest. This was a gray area. I sensed the officer was reluctant to make the arrest.

"Could I explain what happened?"

"I'm listening," he said.

I told him I wasn't trying to shoot the man. I shot the man's tires.

"A man may feel personally threatened when somebody is shooting his tires," he said.

"If I had meant him any personal harm there was little to prevent me from inflicting it," I said.

He nodded.

I told him about the trash problem along my road frontage. I told him about the man in the truck illegally dumping trash. He stopped me again. "Are you aware the man had permission from the owner of the property to dump the trash?"

This statement hit me like a hammer. Not once had I thought of this.

Meekly, I said, "No, I was not aware . . . is there anything I can do?"

"What are you willing to do?"

"This is not only embarrassing – it could cost me my job. It could have a profound effect on my children. I will do whatever it takes."

"Let me talk to the man."

*Skating too close to the edge.*

He left me standing in my driveway.

Before my daughter came home from school, the officer returned and presented me with a $600 bill for three new truck tires. I gladly paid it.

For some time, this near-disaster weighed heavily on my mind. All my life I felt I had a circuit breaker that tripped before my hair caught fire. This all had failed me. The warning signs were there and I had not seen them – I was Quincy Fowler with a chicken on my front porch.

I decided I needed an attitude adjustment. I would not stop skating near the edge, but I would move my fence back so I could see the edge, but not over the edge.

The next year my younger daughter went to a prep school in Virginia. With my more civilized attitude and no children left at home, I was ready to move back east.

# ≡ CHAPTER 18 ≡

## NEVER LET THEM SEE YOU SWEAT

*There is nothing so agonizing to the fine skin
of vanity as the application of a rough truth.*

—EDWARD G. BULWER-LYTTON 1803-1873, BRITISH NOVELIST

*L-1011 TriStar lifting off from Portland, Oregon.*

1994: ATLANTA (ATL), GEORGIA — A co-pilot may run to a flight to save time when switching airplanes. An engineer may get dirty and sweaty while investigating a maintenance problem. But the captain must never look stressed or in a hurry. The image of calm authority presented by an airline captain is an important part of the job. The captain is in sole command of his ship; neither the passengers nor the crew want to think he cannot handle any situation with cool dispatch. He must always appear in control. He does not run and he does not sweat.

Movie directors show pilots flying in stressful conditions in a state of accelerated agitation. This is probably an unrealistic depiction even though it emphasizes the drama. Once while flying in Vietnam, I listened to the full radio communication with a pilot flying a plane whose fuel tanks had been punctured by ground fire. He was talking to a Saigon controller who was trying to vector him home. He set his course for the airport but told them ahead of time that he didn't think he would make it. He never raised his voice and talked in a dull monotone as if he were discussing what he had eaten for breakfast. His last words were, "I appreciate all your help. I'm not going to make it. See you guys around."

Captain Blankenship of Delta Air Lines exhibited this pilot I-have-it-under-control demeanor. I did not witness his story but it was told to me by a flight attendant who saw the episode first hand while working the business class section on his trip. The fact that some people viewed the good captain as a little prudish caused the story to circulate widely. Blankenship is not the captain's real name.

The first story tells what happened to me. After you read it you will understand why I believe the next story about Captain Blankenship to be true.

As captain on a Delta L-1011 TriStar, I had departed Atlanta for Frankfurt, Germany. About two hours into the flight, during the cabin meal service, I left my seat for one of the two lavatories that served the business class passengers. The lavatories were located at the bulkhead between the front galley and the business class section, up front and in clear view of the passengers.

I put on my hat as I left the cockpit. The hat, having the necessary gold-braided scrambled eggs on the bill, is part of the image in case the captain needs to display his authority while out of the cockpit.

I greeted several passengers on my way to the lavatory. Noting that the occupied sign was not lit up, I reached for the doorknob, and opened the door toward me.

There was a lady seated inside who had forgotten to lock the door. As soon as the doorknob turned she realized her mistake and lunged to catch it, but the door was now moving away as fast as her hand was grasping for it. She came halfway out of the lavatory and was stopped when she ran into my chest. It all happened so fast that I could not avert my eyes before I noticed all of her lower garments were around her ankles. While profusely apologizing, I pushed her and the door back in until it latched.

Red-faced, I turned to see if anyone had witnessed the episode. Everyone in business class was looking at me. By the looks on their faces, I imagined they thought it was my fault – after all, I was the captain; I did have the hat with the scrambled eggs on the bill. How could I not know that she was in there?

Not long after my incident, Captain Blankenship had a similar, but more embarrassing, encounter at the same lavatory on his L-1011 trip to Europe. Tall, silver-haired and deep-voiced, he had a commanding, though humorless, presence. He was formal in the way he managed his airplane and crew – everything by the book. In addition to wearing his hat, he also sometimes wore his captain's coat when leaving the cockpit.

While in cruise, as I had done, Captain Blankenship released his seatbelt and told his co-pilot he was going to the lavatory. He donned his hat with the scrambled eggs on the bill and this time chose to wear his coat, the four stripes and wings giving further evidence of his command authority. Business class was full, and he gave a dignified nod to several seated passengers as he reached for the lavatory door. With his eyes on the passengers and his hand on the doorknob, he opened the door.

The lady in the lavatory was not as lucky as my lady. Because of his momentary distraction, Captain Blankenship did not see her reaching for the doorknob as the door was pulled away from her. She lost her balance, falling forward into the aisle, naked from the waist down. In a futile attempt, he tried to save the situation but lost his balance. To keep from falling, he stepped forward, planting his foot squarely in the tangle of undergarments around the woman's ankles. He did this at the same moment she was trying to get up, which caused him to lose his balance entirely and fall on top of her, knocking his hat off his head.

It was now impossible for either of them to stand and the

commotion had drawn the attention of the entire business class section. For those that had looked on late, it might have appeared the good captain was ravaging the woman. In order to separate himself from the panicked lady, Captain Blankenship had to roll off and reach over her nakedness to untangle his foot. At the same time he reached for his foot the lady was struggling to pull up her garments. It appeared as if they were fighting over the clothes bunched around her ankles.

When at last they separated, the lady disappeared into the lavatory. Captain Blankenship stood; his hat with the scrambled eggs had rolled under a nearby seat, and his normally neatly combed white hair was going in every direction. He gave a wild look and disappeared into the cockpit, leaving for later whatever business he had in the lavatory, and his hat under the business class seat.

# PART 5

RETIRED

# ≡ CHAPTER 19 ≡
## JUST ME AND SCRAGG

*O' God thy sea is so great and my boat is so small.*

—BRETON FISHERMAN'S PRAYER

*Tommy and me aboard Scragg, departing Charleston for Bermuda.*

1999: HAMILTON, MAIN ISLAND, BERMUDA — Against the advice of my friends, the rules of the U.S. Coast Guard and the pleadings of my wife, I was alone on Scragg, my 37-foot sailboat, as the last trace of Bermuda melted off my stern and 900 miles of open sea lay ahead. My good friend, Tom Williams, had sailed with me on the adventure over from Charleston, but halfway through our trip we had become becalmed in the Sargasso Sea. We ran the engine for two days with the uneasy knowledge that we did not have enough fuel to motor the entire way.

On the second day the engine vibrated and our speed went to zero. I tried reversing the prop with the same results. Some giant underwater hand was holding us. I killed the engine, tied a line around my waist and donned a snorkel mask. As I went over the side, I had an eerie feeling knowing there were two miles of water beneath me.

The boat had become entangled in a huge fish net, some of it wrapped tightly around the prop. It was getting dark, so we had to wait in place all night before we could do anything.

At first light, I worked with a knife, trying to cut through the tangle. It was laborious and exhausting work, and we were mindful that the seas could roughen anytime, and if they did, it would be impossible to work under the boat. Finally, just as the wind resumed, I cut away the last of the net. We had an uneventful trip the rest of the way, but it took nine days in total to reach Bermuda.

Because our trip had taken longer than planned, Tommy needed to return immediately. He took the first flight back to the States from Bermuda. I told him I would follow on a later flight after I secured a safe mooring for *Scragg*. Instead, I made a detailed study of the weather charts inside the customs house and decided this was my chance. I would sail back single-handed. I spent the night at the customs dock, and the following morning I departed – just me and *Scragg*.

Being alone at sea is unlike being alone anywhere else. I have spent days by myself in the woods, but it isn't the same. We were not born creatures of the sea and do not survive long without a boat. The sea is volatile and unpredictable, and I have always feared it. It does not care if you have a good excuse for the predicament you find yourself in or whether you are right or wrong. You either survive or you don't, but the sea rolls on, and thousands of years from now it will still roll on. If you show extreme courage when it unleashes its fury it gives no credit, and when you are alone there is nothing and no one to sing your praises. If you sink, except for its inhabitants feeding on your remains, to the sea you never existed.

When I was eight years old, I saw the ocean for the first time. We had moved to Charleston from western North Carolina, and my first view was at Folly Beach. On our drive down Folly Road, the morose silence of the Spanish moss answered the whisper of a gentle breeze – the smell of the salt air and marsh heightened my anticipation – then I could hear the low steady roar. When I walked out on the beach it was exciting, but I also experienced an underlying foreboding.

In my youth, I worked as a lifeguard at the Isle of Palms Beach for four years. I spent untold hours gazing at the undulating swells, the breaking waves, the advancing and receding foam. I witnessed its power when it took the life of a young father during a storm. And yet, the more I felt its mystery and might, the more I was drawn to it.

For 30 years, I sailed off and on. And for about four years, I gradually worked to equip my sailboat so I could operate it alone. I had successfully mastered the requirements and been awarded a U.S. Coast Guard Captain's License and had sailed the seas many times with a companion.

So why sail alone? Technically, it was against regulations since a lookout was always required. For years I read about sailing, and though it was not directly condoned, the implication was that you haven't looked Neptune in the eye unless you've done it alone. There was something added to the challenge if there was no companion to help with either information or brawn. It was you against this unforgiving, timeless, unfathomable enigma, and although there are great sailors who never go alone, the true tempter of fate is the single-handed sailor.

For the first two days after leaving Bermuda, I had a comfortable 15 knots of wind. I was working a close reach in gentle seas while steering with a Monitor wind vane that operated flawlessly. It required no electrical power and very little attention, so long as the wind direction remained constant.

Two hours before sunset on the second day the wind quit. I ran the engine for the next hour and a half, as the sea's calm image became increasingly serene. After an hour of motoring, the ocean had not the slightest ripple and from horizon to horizon it was as if I were traveling across a gigantic mirror. As the sun set, the sky turned blood red in the west, and then the sea itself turned red. I stopped the engine and sat motionless in what appeared to be a sea of blood. From high above, I have viewed the snow-capped Alps, the Grand Canyon and Yosemite – watched the dancing curtain of colors in the aurora and looked down on the glaciers of Greenland. I have seen the green flash just as the setting sun disappeared into the horizon – looked through the frenetic prancing of Saint Elmo's fire on the cockpit windows while flying through weather. In command of a flying machine, I have threaded my way through giant thunderstorms on a summer evening and witnessed their symphony of lights. But nothing matched the reverence I felt watching that sunset, as I sat motionless on a glassy blood-red sea. There was not a sound, not even small lapping noises on the side of the boat – only me and my insignificant little boat suspended in a vast red world. I did not move until the sun set and the red faded.

I usually assess situations in light of the earthly facts involved, but being alone in the vastness of the universe challenged my mind to consider the possibility of an unseen force. With no mate to check my thoughts, I could imagine the ocean of blood was an omen of my doom.

Later that night the wind gradually returned, so I raised the sails and was once again making good time. All the next day the wind was a constant 18 knots. Stretched out on the stern locker, I could see the boat wake on the starboard side and the ocean out front. I was sailing pleasantly at seven knots and thoughts of the blood-sea receded.

When danger appears with no warning, sometimes there is a delay before the true seriousness of the threat is realized. Once I was walking in the woods several miles from civilization, I looked down and discovered I was straddling a cotton mouth moccasin. Armed with a shotgun, I very slowly pointed the muzzle between my legs and fired. The trauma didn't set in until I began to weigh the possibilities. These same emotions slowly evolved as *Scragg* sped by a 50-foot pole, missing us by five feet. A little to the left and it would have holed *Scragg*, and the boat surely would have sunk. Was this another omen, or had I just escaped the prophecy of the blood-sea?

Later that same day, while asleep, a loud noise and a sharp lurching of the boat awakened me. The cockpit was full of water and the sails were wet over halfway up the mast. Looking around I saw a giant wave receding off the starboard side. The cockpit quickly drained, and the steering vane brought her back to course. *Scragg* had taken the rogue wave in stride, but I wondered about the omen of the blood sea.

On the third day the wind freshened to 20 knots. I took a single reef in the main and shortened the jib on the roller furling. The reduced sail worked well, and *Scragg* performed beautifully. It should be noted that I had invested a great deal of thought and time in rigging the boat so I could work everything from the cockpit since the deck in bad weather is a dangerous place to be.

The wind had shifted from a more westerly direction, and after some calculation, I determined that I could not make Charleston on my present tack. I still had the Gulf Stream to cross, and the northbound current would push me even further off course. To get to Charleston, it would be necessary to change tack several times, and I would be forced to sail on a less comfortable beat. This would probably require two extra days, and I was concerned about the hurricane risk. Twice each day I contacted a weather mapping station on my HF radio and pulled up a weather map through my computer. At the time, there was no storm activity in the Atlantic, but it was July, and the possibility existed.

I changed my plans and set sail for Beaufort, North Carolina. This would result in an easier and shorter ride, although it did produce a new concern for navigation. Off the coast of Beaufort is Cape Lookout, with its infamous reefs. I would need to navigate to the south and then come in on the inside of the reef, but not too far south because of another dangerous reef called Frying Pan Shoals.

After dark, and with all systems performing well under the stronger wind, I went below for a three-hour nap. During the times I slept below, the radar was positioned so I could see it from my bunk. The alarm circle was set for five miles, so if a ship came within this circle, I would be awakened.

About two hours later, I awoke to an increase in wind and sea noise with more boat motion. The boat was heeling in excess, and the wind steering vane was working hard to maintain course. Looking through the companionway, I could see the cockpit taking in water from breaking waves. The wind speed had increased to 30 knots, and the waves were larger, but in the dark I couldn't see their actual size.

The sail area had to be reduced, and quick. The strain on the rigging was huge, to say nothing of the uncomfortable sailing conditions. I snapped on my safety harness, the tether fitting always left hanging over the steps to the companionway. Once in the cockpit, I surveyed the situation. This was it – this was what the challenge was all about. If I messed this up, I would be in big trouble. I dared not set up a situation where I was required to go out on deck. The waves were breaking over the deck; the boat listed in excess of 30 degrees; and the sails, the fitting, and the rigging creaked and groaned. Control of the jib would be lost if the roller furling failed, the sheet line failed or the furling line failed. If there was a failure in a shroud, the backstay, or the headstay, the mast would break and everything would come down.

I first eased into the wind and rolled up the jib to about half of what I had out. Then, I went over my cockpit reefing procedures for the main. This required heading into the wind and operating a combination of three cleats and three winches. The whole process worked as planned, and *Scragg* was soon back on course sailing much more comfortably at hull speed under a double reef.

Perhaps it should be explained that each displacement boat has its own hull speed, which is determined by the waterline length of the boat. Beyond the hull speed the drag increases to the point that the boat would need to plane on top in order to go faster, although it can exceed the hull speed for short durations in heavy weather. An airplane designed for subsonic flight has a similar limitation. In the airplane, drag greatly increases as sound speed is approached. Both airplane and boat can approach these thresholds routinely, and without much stress, but not go beyond them. *Scragg* had a hull speed of slightly more than seven knots.

After my test administered by Mother Nature, I was wet, cold and very tired. So after checking everything again, I went below to sleep.

The next morning the wind was still blowing at 25 knots. The waves were large, but both man and boat were in their element – at their peak. *Scragg* was a Pacific Seacraft, Crelock 37, and one of the finest ocean sailing vessels ever built.

In spite of the rough conditions, I managed to drink about as much coffee as I spilled. After a power bar and a piece of cheese I felt wonderful. I was over halfway to Beaufort. The night before, I had risen to the challenge, was sailing in heavy seas at maximum boat speed, and, as of yet this morning, I wasn't sick. Sick? Yes, sick.

Even though I have had a lifetime of motion, I have been plagued by motion sickness since childhood. As a five-year-old, I would get sick in a swing and in the car on the switchback road to my grandmother's house in the mountains. At the county fair, I got sick on the rides.

At age 14, I had a six-week job working on a charter fishing boat. I ran the ship's galley, located on deck with easy access to the side rail where I could also assist with the fishing. Once I was making sandwiches for two hotshot Yankee tourists when the subject of seasickness was discussed. The boat was rolling smartly, and I was starting to notice that all-too-familiar feeling coming on. One of them turned to me and said, "I bet you have seen a lot of these women getting sick in this kind of sea?"

"Well . . . uh, yes sir, but men get sick, too."

"I guess they do, if they got a weak stomach and never been out before."

I quickly turned to the man and said, "Excuse me," and I ran to the side and threw up.

They looked at me for a few seconds, looked at each other and walked away, leaving their sandwiches.

I learned to fly in a J-3 cub when I was still in high school. My instructor had shown me how to do spins, and even though I was told not to practice them solo, it was my nature to push the limits. I would make myself sick, open the window and attempt to throw up outside. After these flights, my disgusted instructor would make me wash the airplane.

When I went through pilot training, the Air Force had just switched to an all jet program. We were required to learn high G maneuvers and aerobatics. Naturally, I got sick, but herein lies part of the reason I persisted at my sailing: I got over motion sickness when flying. If I could get over it while flying, I could get over it at sea.

So, along with my success in mastering the skills of single-handed sailing, my elation on this fourth day also stemmed from the fact that I was sailing in rough weather with no medication, and I wasn't sick.

I rigged my extension stereo speakers for cockpit listening, put on the soundtrack from "Top Gun" and cranked up the volume. *Scragg* sliced through the big waves with the grace and courage of a matador. Salt spray stung my face as the music blared – *take it right into the danger zone – out on the edge is where I always yearn to be.* I had that feeling, that soaring euphoria that comes from being in synch with nature and my machine. For the first time since retiring – that feeling of Delta's big jet roaring into the air, pushed by 180,000 pounds of thrust as I lift off for a foreign land; that feeling of being upside down in the slot doing 500 knots in an Air Force jet, six feet from the exhaust of my lead aircraft, convinced nothing can shake me from his tail – my pulse 180, the cockpit at 60 degrees, and my flight suit soaking wet – I AM THE MASTER!

I had conquered Mother Nature – I was in command. I threw my hands to the heavens and shouted my ecstasy.

Arrogance seldom goes unpunished, and at sea, punishment can be severe.

By nightfall, I was very tired. I logged my position and fine-tuned my course for crossing the Gulf Stream. Up until then I had not seen another vessel, but I knew the northbound ship traffic liked to take advantage of the fuel and time saved by the Gulf Stream current. I turned on my radar, set the target alarm and instantly fell asleep.

*Under a double reef in heavy seas.*

Around midnight the radar alarm went off. I got up and quickly lined up the radar cursor to determine the direction of relative motion. After watching for a few minutes, I realized whatever was out there was on a collision course with *Scragg*. The relative line of motion was about 60 degrees to the port side of my course. This line is determined by the speed and heading of the converging vessel along with my own speed and heading. I guessed his speed to be greater than mine so his heading was probably around 20 or 30 degrees. My course at this time was 290 degrees. My masthead light was not on, indicating I was under sail. The target had to be looking at my red sidelight. In both cases, I was the stand-on vessel and, by international rules he should make an evasive turn. When it did not appear he was going to give way, I tried to contact him on the VHF radio.

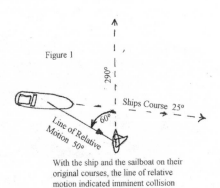

With the ship and the sailboat on their original courses, the line of relative motion indicated imminent collision

By now I had moved to the cockpit and was looking at the green sidelight of what appeared, from its other lights, to be a small freighter. There was still no response to my radio calls. When it was clear a collision was imminent, I turned my boat to starboard, away from the wind. While in this turn, I heard a response on the VHF, in broken English, "I see you now."

I continued in the turn until I had reversed course. Now I had backed my sails and was doing only 2 knots.

To my astonishment, we were still on a collision course and very close. I was aghast and perplexed. What was going on? In a last desperate effort, I requested the ship's heading. The reply was "0-6-0." I demanded, "Turn starboard 1-2-0 to avoid collision."

"But I see your green," he replied.

Dismayed, I shouted into the radio mic, "Turn starboard 1-2-0 to avoid collision."

I saw his turn slowly progressing as he passed within 25 yards of *Scragg* At the same time that I had requested the target turn to starboard, I started a turn to port, but I was powered with the wind on the wrong side of my sails, and the response was agonizingly slow. We started to separate. Now I know the emotions of having the noose around your neck when the pardon arrives.

It was some time before I figured out what had happened. Evidently, just as I started my first turn to reverse course, the ship's helmsman had finally seen me and took corrective action by turning to starboard. This was when he announced, "I see you now." Further evidence of this was when he stated his heading was 0-6-0. This heading had to be a change, because it would not have put the ship on a collision course when I was tracking it on radar. When he stated, "But I see your green," it was because I had reversed course, and now I appeared to be the give-way vessel. He was confused, because he had just seen my red when he first spotted me and made his turn. We both had changed direction to create a new collision course. Because it was dark, we were too confused to understand what was happening. (See illustrations.)

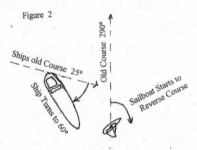

Just as sailboat starts to reverse course ship sees
it and takes evasive action by turning to 60°

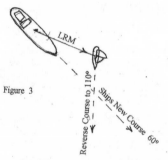

With sailboat on new course of 110° and
ship on new course of 60° the line of relative
motion puts them on a new collision course

Neither of us spoke again, but just as I was being liberated from my burial at sea, I clearly heard a radio transmission from another ship chastising me for my radio procedures. Since I had entered the Gulf Stream, there were other ships just over the horizon, which

I could not see. I heard a radio call from somebody in very good English: "This channel is reserved for safety, how about holding down the chatter."

CHATTER? The fool, I almost died. This deserved an answer, but I was too shaken to bother.

I arrived in Beaufort early on the sixth day. Other than being apprehensive about navigating at night between Cape Fear and Cape Lookout, both infamous spots for shipwrecks, the rest of my trip was pleasant. As I motored on the calm waters of the harbor, I reflected on my single-handed challenge at sea. I was pleased that I had done it but felt somewhat subdued. Yes, I had looked Neptune in the eye, but I think I may have blinked.

I kept *Scragg* for five more years, and she served me well, but I found that I was sailing her less, and sometimes I dreaded the work needed to keep her going. The day I sold her was a sad day. With a lump in my throat, I waited on board while the closing took place, hoping something would go wrong, and the sale would fall through. Just as it is with a good hunting dog, I had love and respect for her. At least I was pleased with the new owner. He was a retired navy vice admiral, and I knew he would appreciate what she was.

So why was she named *Scragg*? The name certainly raised eyebrows on the boating communications network. When I was at The Citadel we sometimes read Al Capp's "L'il Abner" in the Sunday comics. The Scraggs were characters who would come out of the hills and attack the local village. They were unkempt and savage, and they had very bad manners. One of my disparaging classmates commented that not only did I act like the Scraggs, but I looked like them. The name stuck. It was supposed to be derogatory, but I liked it.

Before my departure from Charleston, my 11-year-old daughter and I prepared messages written in English, French and Spanish. They asked for a return response and contained our e-mail address, phone number, and home address. On the trip to Bermuda, I took five small plastic water bottles and sealed the messages inside. As we crossed the Gulf Stream, we tossed a bottle overboard at every degree change of longitude.

One year after my Bermuda trip, my daughter received an e-mail from Ireland. A 12-year-old girl had found one of our bottles on a lonely western beach in the southern part of Ireland (see insert). But for the separation of a few feet from either the floating piling or the freighter, that message could have been the last communication from *Scragg* and me.

*And the timeless unforgiving sea rolls on.*

Subj: **Bottles at sea.**
Date: 8/14/00 6:19:59 PM Eastern Daylight Time
From: PRUNTYS@INDIGO.IE (PRUNTY A & J)
To: nbeirne@aol.com

Ms Mary Beirne Taylor.
Your bottle turned up on the west coast of Ireland if you get this message I will give you all the details by return.
Yours Sincerely .
John Prunty.

<!DOCTYPE HTML PUBLIC "-//W3C//DTD W3 HTML//EN">

<HEAD>

<META content=text/html;charset=iso-8859-1 http-equiv=Content-Type>
<META content="MSHTML 4.72.3110.7" name=GENERATOR>
</HEAD>

<DIV>Ms Mary Beirne Taylor.</DIV>
<DIV>Your bottle turned up on the west coast of
Ireland if you get this message I will give you all the details by
return.</DIV>
<DIV>Yours Sincerely .</DIV>
<DIV>John Prunty.</DIV>

———————— Headers ————————
Return-Path: <PRUNTYS@INDIGO.IE>
Received: from rly-zb04.mx.aol.com (rly-zb04.mail.aol.com [172.31.41.4]) by air-zb05.mail.aol.com (v75_b3.11) with ESMTP
Mon, 14 Aug 2000 18:19:59 -0400
Received: from relay05.indigo.ie (relay05.indigo.ie [194.125.133.229]) by rly-zb04.mx.aol.com (v75_b3.9) with ESMTP; Mon,
14 Aug 2000 18:19:39 -0400
Received: (qmail 18852 messnum 1190528 invoked from network[194.125.205.208/ts08-081.dublin.indigo.ie]); 14 Aug 2000
22:19:33 -0000
Received: from ts08-081.dublin.indigo.ie (HELO oemcomputer) (194.125.205.208)
  by relay05.indigo.ie (qp 18852) with SMTP; 14 Aug 2000 22:19:33 -0000
Message-ID: <001701c0063e$ee127560$d0cd7dc2@oemcomputer>
From: "PRUNTY A & J" <PRUNTYS@INDIGO.IE>
To: <nbeirne@aol.com>
Subject: Bottles at sea.
Date: Mon, 14 Aug 2000 23:28:07 +0100
MIME-Version: 1.0
Content-Type: multipart/alternative;
    boundary="—-=_NextPart_000_0014_01C00647.4D484340"
X-Priority: 3
X-MSMail-Priority: Normal
X-Mailer: Microsoft Outlook Express 4.72.3110.1
X-MimeOLE: Produced By Microsoft MimeOLE V4.72.3110.3

187

Subj:   **Fw: Fw: bottles on the beech.**
Date:   8/21/00 12:21:31 PM Eastern Daylight Time
From:   PRUNTYS@INDIGO.IE (PRUNTY A & J)
To: nbeirne@aol.com

——Original Message——
From: PRUNTY A & J <PRUNTYS@INDIGO.IE>
To: Nbeirne@aol.com <Nbeirne@aol.com>
Date: 21 August 2000 17:29
Subject: Re: Fw: bottles on the beech.

>Hi Mary.
>Thank you for your email.
>My daughter and I were walking on the beech it was a beautiful sunny day
>that is how we spotted the bottle,glisten in the sun. We found it on the
>12/8/2000, It was at a little place called Spanish Point [ The Spanish
>Armada was wrecked there in 1886 coming to the aid of Irish rebellion hence
>the name]  that is on the west coast of Ireland If we go any further we
>would end up in New York. My daughter is 12 years old and this is quiet an
>adventure for her.
>Thank you .
>John Prunty.
>——Original Message——
>From: Nbeirne@aol.com <Nbeirne@aol.com>
>To: PRUNTYS@indigo.ie <PRUNTYS@indigo.ie>
>Date: 20 August 2000 00:30
>Subject: Re: Fw: bottles on the beech.
>
>
>>Dear John Prunty,
>>Hi. I am very excited that you found the bottle.  I didn't think it would
>>reach anyone.  My dad sailed from Charleston to Bermuda around the 4th of
>>July in 1999.  My dad threw most of the bottles out around the gulf
stream.
>>He threw them out and I wrote the letters and thought of the idea. I am 11
>>years old.
>>    If you tell me the number I can tell you the longitude and lattidude
of
>>where the bottle was thrown out.
>>    Where did you find the bottle?? When??
>>
>>          from,
>>     Mary Beirne Taylor
>>
>

————————— Headers —————————
Return-Path: <PRUNTYS@INDIGO.IE>
Received: from rly-yb01.mx.aol.com (rly-yb01.mail.aol.com [172.18.146.1]) by air-yb01.mail.aol.com (v75_b3.11) with
ESMTP; Mon, 21 Aug 2000 12:21:30 -0400
Received: from relay06.indigo.ie (relay06.indigo.ie [194.125.133.230]) by rly-yb01.mx.aol.com (v75_b3.9) with ESMTP; Mon,
21 Aug 2000 12:21:09 -0400

# ≡ CHAPTER 20 ≡
## ATMOS

*It is possible to fail in many ways . . . while to succeed is possible only in one way.*

—ARISTOTLE (NICOMACHEAN ETHICS)

1955 & 2007: CHARLESTON, SOUTH CAROLINA — March 31,
Peter Simmons was dead. "Retired Negro Blacksmith Dies in Mt.
Pleasant . . . ." I read the small article in the two-week-old 1955
*News & Courier*. My father had come across the article as he was
disposing of his saved reading material. There had been no mention of his death by anybody I knew. Why should there be? Even
though he had been the master of his craft, both he and his craft
were of another era. And though he was the teacher and mentor of
the now famous iron working artisan, Philip Simmons, that light
would not shine for another 50 years.

Peter Simmons was dead; he was buried, and my debt had gone
unpaid.

Two years prior to Peter's death, I was a rebellious, reluctant and
often absent student at General William Moultrie High School in
Mt. Pleasant, South Carolina. I often missed school for no other
reason than feeling a need to roam the countryside with my dog
and gun. At this time it became my good fortune to contract
whooping cough. I say *good* fortune because this was a contagious
disease, and I was forbidden to attend school for not less than two
weeks or the duration of the disease.

While I knew little of *Paradise Lost, Julius Caesar* or conjugat-
ing verbs, I could talk at length about the mid-range trajectory and
sectional density of a 130-grain bullet fired from a 270 Winchester
at 3,050 feet per second, or the length and weight of the knife used
by Jim Bowie at the Alamo. I had read about the art of making
knives and wanted to try my hand at it.

The whooping cough put me down for only a few days, leaving me nearly two weeks to start my knife. First, I needed a good grinding wheel, which we did not have, and I could not afford. In exploring the loft of the barn, I found a broken water pump with a good three-quarter-horse motor attached. Before mounting the motor to my workbench, I needed to find a shaft adapter to attach the grinding wheel.

Coleman's Hardware was the one place I knew that if a part could be found that would work it would be there. Besides, I loved going there. The smell of sweet molasses feed, new metal and lubricating oils was as distinct and familiar as the people who ran the place. The front of the building had every hardware item man could want and things he did not know he wanted until he discovered them there. I sometimes daydreamed about attaching one piece of hardware to another to make a new invention.

Colorful bags of livestock feed were stacked in the back of the building. This is where I picked out the material for my mother to fashion my new shirts. Puberty brings more testosterone, and with some work, testosterone brings more muscles. Once formed, there exists a need to subtly display these muscles. On my instructions, my mother tailored the feed sack shirts to display this developing machismo. This tailoring, along with the bold colors and patterns on the feed sacks, produced custom shirts that earned the envy of my friends. Coleman's Hardware was where I bought my ammunition, where we found miscellaneous farm items, and where I found the shaft adapter for attaching the grinding wheel to my old pump motor.

Now it was time to find the right steel for the knife blade. While reading knife books instead of school books, I had learned about carbon content and heat tempering. The secret was to have a blade that was hard enough to hold an edge but not so hard as to be brittle. The type of steel and how fast it was allowed to cool after being heated would determine this characteristic. I first experimented with several large old files. I built a fire pit and heated them in it until they turned cherry-red, but even after this re-tempering, they still were too hard.

Upon further research, I discovered the steel that would be perfect. Automobiles in those days usually had springs made from stacking decreasing lengths of steel of about two inches wide and one quarter inch thick. These were made from excellent metal that was not brittle but was still hard. I found my steel springs while rummaging through the junk thrown out by a local car repair shop.

I built a fire in the pit and heated the spring steel, straightened it and put it back into the hot coals to cool very slowly. This would produce the softest steel for shaping the knife on the grinding wheel. I became so immersed in my project that I did not want to stop to eat or do my chores. I certainly did not want to return to school.

Many hours of working on my homemade grinding wheel produced a beautifully shaped, twelve-inch Bowie knife. I was now ready to practice the delicate art of heating and cooling to obtain the perfect temper. With the extra pieces of spring, I practiced at my makeshift forge, but I was not satisfied with the results. I knew that plunging the blade into water would cause it to cool too fast. I tried cooling in motor oil, transmission fluid and even very thick gear oil. These experiments did improve the temper, but not to my satisfaction.

By now, the usual amount of time required away from school for whooping cough quarantine had expired, but I was too engrossed with the project to quit. I knew the rules required that students be cough-free before returning to school. With some practice, I developed a convincing cough and was able to avoid returning to school for a few days longer. I continued to experiment even after I was compelled to return to school, I spent my afternoons until dark working on the perfect knife.

When all of my experimentation failed to find the correct temper for my knife, I returned to Coleman's Hardware and asked for advice. I was told there was an old black man who had been the last working blacksmith in Mt. Pleasant. But they cautioned me that he was more than ninety years old and no longer did much work.

Peter Simmons lived in a small well-kept house on the edge of the Old Village. I was apprehensive as I knocked on his door. A middle-aged black woman came to the door, and I asked to speak to Mr. Peter Simmons. She frowned and cocked her head slightly. "He aine heah."

My father's oil business served much of the black community, and his name was well regarded. I quickly told her who I was, explaining I was looking for blacksmith advice, and she seemed to relax. She nodded and told me to wait for a moment.

The man who came to the door had a full head of hair white as cotton and a small white mustache. In spite of his age, he stood tall and straight. His face was swamp-water black, deeply lined, like the smoky forge had seasoned him. He bore no expression, and, like the woman, he stood quietly waiting for me to speak.

Unsure of myself, I presented my knife and tried to explain my problem. He listened, and, for awhile, said nothing. When he spoke, I was not sure if it was a riddle, poetry or blacksmith talk. I started again to explain myself, "Mr. Simmons –"

He put up his hand and stopped me before I could say anything more.

"I'ze been Peter for 96 years and when you wants sump'um I'ze still Peter."

I began again, "Peter, I have tried tempering with several kinds of oil and even gear oil and my knife is still too hard and – "

He stopped me again with this confounding statement: "Atmos, young man, you needs Atmos."

"Sir?"

"Don't call me, sir. For 96 years, I'ze been Peter and I'ze Peter to you now."

"Peter, how can I temper my knife?"

"Atmos," he said again. "Atmos give you life. You tempers by atmos. Come."

He led me through the house and out the back door to his blacksmith shop. Everything about the place was old, musty and rusted. To my surprise, Peter soon had the forge glowing hot. He picked up my knife with scarred and callused hands, the skin on the top stretched loose like it no longer fit.

I thought he would put the knife in the forge, but instead he walked to a piled jumble of metal scraps and picked out a piece of baling wire about ten feet long. He threaded the wire through the hole I had drilled in the knife for the handle attachment and placed the blade in the forge. When the metal was red hot, he handed me the other end of the wire and demonstrated how I should swing the knife around my head in a large circle. Using the tongs to remove the knife, he held it up for me. As I swung the knife, he said, "Atmos, tempered by atmos."

Now I understood. Atmosphere! The swinging allowed the air to cool it slower than dipping it in oil but faster than just letting it sit. After Peter motioned me to stop swinging the blade, he let it cool, then picked it up and disengaged the wire.

"How much do I owe you?" I asked.

"Money cannot buy what's you owe," he replied. "When I die, I wants you to pick a single leaf from a live oak tree and before they puts me in the ground you comes to me in my box. You takes that leaf and places it on my chest and says to me, 'Peter, I leave this as a token to you.'"

I promised I would, then thanked him and left.


Peter's tempering proved to be the perfect method to harden the type of steel in my knife. He had been a blacksmith for so long that he could divine the nature of any metal he worked. I have thrown it at trees and never damaged the blade and yet it will hold an edge like a razor . . . "The touch of the master's hand." Peter had done me right and now it was too late to pay an honest debt.

But remorse faded as life accelerated. I graduated from The Citadel, became an Air Force pilot and went to war. Through the

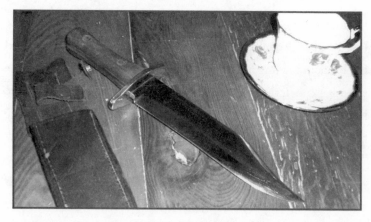

*The finished knife.*

many years of flying for Delta Air Lines I did not forget Peter entirely. I remembered him and felt a slight twinge of guilt every time I touched the custom knife in my gun case.

Ten years after retiring as a pilot with Delta Air Lines, I was visiting the old brick rail station in downtown Charleston that had been converted to a visitor center. Hanging on the wall was a portrait of an old black man. A plaque nearby indicated the man in the portrait was the blacksmith named Philip Simmons. Could this be Peter's son? I learned that even though they shared the same last name and Philip had been an apprentice under Peter for years, they were not related. Philip had by then received considerable recognition for his artistic ironwork around Charleston. Philip Simmons' picture reminded me of Peter, and it was not long before I was thinking again about my unpaid debt.

Next to the village of Mt. Pleasant is a beautiful old cemetery that served both the white and the black community in the 1950s. A wide path called Hallelujah Lane divides the sections. The black section is known as Ocean View, and the white as Ocean Grove, though the ocean cannot be seen from either side. I walked all over a poorly kept section of Ocean View in search of Peter's name, but many headstones were missing, and I did not find it.

On my next trip to Charleston, I continued my search at the Lutheran church, which manages Ocean Grove cemetery. I asked to see a plat map of the gravesites, but was told that town records from the 1950s had been destroyed by fire. They suggested I try the African Methodist Episcopal Church (AME) on Royall Avenue. But the AME Church did not have records either. They sent me to Johnson & Halls Funeral home, the only black funeral home at the time of Peter's death. But they had no records either. Once again I postponed my search until a later date.

When I arrived in Charleston for my next attempt, I talked to Philip Simmons around the time of his ninety-fourth birthday, an age very close to that of Peter's when he had helped me with my knife more than fifty years before. Philip recalled that he had attended Peter's funeral at Ocean View, though did not recall the location of the burial spot. He talked some about his apprenticeship and said that Peter had turned over the blacksmith business to him.

From the AME Church, I got the names of Maggie Brown and Johannah Gold, who might have knowledge of Peter's gravesite. Johannah had a picture of him and Maggie knew of a grandson living in Texas and helped me track him down. The grandson gave me a copy of the death certificate, which identified Ocean View as the place of burial. Meanwhile, Maggie made an exhaustive search of the cemetery and called me after I returned to Atlanta to let me know that she thought Peter's grave was unmarked. There was no way I could place an oak leaf on his grave, but I was still determined to pay my debt.

Fifty-four years after I made my promise to Peter Simmons, I placed a memorial stone in the cemetery where he was buried, beneath the canopy of a live oak. Under a single oak leaf cut into the stone, the inscription reads:

PETER SIMMONS

MASTER BLACKSMITH

DEC 25, 1856

MARCH 31, 1955

*Peter, I leave this as a token to you. I promised I would.*

# CHAPTER 21

## WILL THE REAL TURKEY PLEASE STAND UP

*True, a little learning is a dangerous thing,*
*but it still beats total ignorance.*

—ABIGAIL VAN BUREN

2006: SOUTH GEORGIA — We had seen and heard turkeys throughout the 2005-06 deer season, so despite the admonitions of experienced turkey hunters about our odds, we were going turkey hunting. Four of us had a 700-acre lease in South Georgia. Although I had been a hunter off and on all my life, I had never pursued the wily bird. My turkey hunting friends regaled me with stories about the difficulties of outsmarting a clever gobbler. Many had hunted for years without bagging one.

My hunting partner and son-in-law, Neal Heery, also had never hunted turkeys. He often gave the appearance of deferring to my hunting knowledge, but I suspected the deference had more to do with my age and position as his father-in-law than my actual hunting prowess. Neal and I had practiced our turkey calling until our wives summarily ended it. The day before the season opened we drove ourselves crazy with more practicing at hunt camp. We tried mouth calls, box calls and slate calls, which only further increased our confusion and provoked arguments about what sounded most authentic. The idea, of course, was to sound just like a horny turkey hen. We had a problem, though. Neither of us knew what a horny hen sounded like.

We loaded the truck an hour before daylight with camo outfits, decoys and camouflaged guns, then drove within half a mile of our selected spot. We walked quietly to a location that had some underbrush that would provide cover, but that still afforded a view of a clearing. One jake (a young male) and two hen decoys were positioned in the clearing. I'd like to say this selection was a function of our evolved turkey hunting knowledge, but I'd be lying.

The selection was random, made when we bought a bunch of other turkey stuff. I had vaguely recalled something about a jake enraging an older gobbler because he was in pursuit of the young virgin hens, and the gobbler, like some men I have known, felt that all of it belonged to him. This story appealed to my sense of order, so I bought a jake.

Behind the decoys the terrain fell off into a wooded area where Neal had heard turkeys the day before. We settled in about 50 yards apart and out of sight of each other. Deciding to use the slate calls, we agreed that I would do most of the calling. Much to my dismay, I discovered I had left my striker back at the truck. I tried to stroke the slate with a carved stick. It sounded more like a sick crow, and Neal begged me to stop. Neal tried calling with his slate, but the striker skipped and scratched like somebody scraping old gravy from a frying pan, and I begged him to stop.

Finally, in disgust, I walked back to the truck to get my striker. By the time I got back, it was full daylight. I concluded that by now any turkey in our area was running for his life, but I decided to settle in anyway and work on my call. Hard as I tried, I couldn't get it right. Somehow it had been easier to sound authentic back at camp. Still, we persevered, but even so we got no better. We each laughed at the other, convinced we sounded about as much like a virgin turkey hen as a blue jay sounded like a duck.

After a while, I became bored and, for no particular reason, leaned around the bushes and looked down the old logging road behind me. Coming up the road at a trot was a big gobbler. I first thought it was my brain playing tricks on me. Quickly, though, I realized it was no mirage. Somehow, one of us or the combination of us had stumbled onto the magic note and we were Pied Pipers floating sweet music to a gobbler hell bent on lustful self-destruction – *come hither – come hither – we are the Angelina Jolies of turkey hens and we are yours.*

He slowed about 30 yards away and went into a full strut, either showing off for the hens or mad at the jake. I could hear my wiser turkey hunting friends warn me that turkeys can see like eagles, run like deer and fly like pheasants. I figured that as soon as I moved into shooting position the gobbler would disappear. I aimed. Just as he came out of the strut I fired, and the great gobbler fell flopping to the ground.

"What are you doing?! Are you OK?" Neal called, sounding very anxious.

"I shot a turkey."

Neal came over with a look of relief on his face, not because he thought I had shot a turkey, but because he was relieved that I had not shot myself. Neal confided to me later that when he heard me shoot he thought, "What a total fiasco. Now the old man has accidentally discharged his gun."

The gobbler was huge with a six-inch beard. I couldn't resist; I called a lawyer friend who had, over the course of 10 years, tried to bag a turkey but never scored. I did my best to sound nonchalant, even off-handed.

"We were out of the woods with our gobbler by nine o'clock," I said. I did not tell him that we hunted hard for the next three days, using every calling combination we could imagine. Some calls even sounded like turkeys, but we didn't see another turkey. We had found the song of sirens for gobblers, but unfortunately, we couldn't remember how to play it again.

*Will the real turkey please stand up.*

# ≡ CHAPTER 22 ≡
## WE LOVE TO FLY AND IT SHOWS

*If a man has a talent and cannot use it, he has failed. If he has a talent and uses only half of it, he has partly failed. If he has a talent and learns somehow to use the whole of it, he has gloriously succeeded, and won a satisfaction and a triumph few men ever know.*

—THOMAS WOLFE (1900-1938)

2013: ATLANTA, GEORGIA — The title of this story was a 1987 Delta Air Lines slogan. It sums up the work ethic during my career, a career that began just as the jet age was taking off and ended at the mandatory retirement age of 60. To work as a pilot for Delta during this period was a privilege unequaled at any other company or job. The employees were happy. They got along with each other, and they wanted their passengers to be happy. At times we went to great lengths to accommodate our customers and even broke rules on their behalf.

As captain on a Boeing 757, I listened to an argument between a flight attendant and a passenger carrying a large painting. According to the passenger, he had been led to believe he could transport his valuable painting on the airplane. The flight attendant explained that he could transport it, but it would need to have special packaging and be carried in the baggage compartment. She stated that it was too large to fit in the overhead bin or even her closet. Of course she was right, but I began to see the passenger's point. He would miss his flight and connection if he went back to the ticket counter to package his painting. I could also tell he was not comfortable with it going in the airplane belly with the other checked bags. Somehow, he had been misled.

I interrupted their discussion. "Give me the painting. I'll take care of it."

I put it in the cockpit behind the jump seat, which was a minor FAA violation. The passenger was exceedingly grateful and probably became a Delta customer for life.

Later I received a tongue-lashing from the flight attendant. She exclaimed that the passengers would never learn if captains overruled them and violated regulations. I ended the conversation with, "Look, I'm sorry I interfered. You are right, but I want you to keep in mind that we are not here to teach rules. We are here to please our passengers so they will return."

I am not normally the type of person who shies away from confrontation. However, as the following situation illustrates, I used imaginative ways to avoid locking horns with my passengers.

At that time smoking was still allowed in the designated section but pipes and cigars were forbidden. A flight attendant entered the Boeing 727 cockpit and reported with a sigh, "We have a Mr. Tartan in first class, a Flying Colonel, and he insists on smoking his pipe. What do you want to do?"

Now this was indeed a ticklish situation. Not only was he flying first class, but he was a Flying Colonel, which meant he was a regular customer that had flown a zillion miles on Delta. After looking out the window a few seconds, I responded. "Okay, I'll take care of it. For now, leave him alone."

Looking at the engineer, I noticed the round outline of a box of Copenhagen dipping tobacco in his shirt pocket. In the past, I had engaged in this nasty habit and knew it packed a kick of nicotine. I borrowed the engineer's snuff, donned my captain's hat and exited the cockpit. Seated next to the window in the last row of the first class section was a distinguished gentleman in a sport coat packing tobacco in his pipe. He looked at me as I sat down next to him. "Mr. Tartan, I'm Captain Taylor. I understand that you and our flight attendant have a misunderstanding over your pipe."

He nodded slightly with just a hint of a smile. "I am in the smoking section, and I smoke a pipe. I have spent thousands of dollars with Delta Airlines, and I think to forbid my habit is ridiculous. Are you aware that I am a Flying Colonel?"

The thought occurred to me that a Flying Colonel would be well aware of the smoking rules. Why he chose my flight to make his stand on pipe smoking was a puzzle. Maybe he wasn't used to being told what to do, and the flight attendant pushed his wrong buttons.

"Yes sir, I am aware that you are a valuable customer for Delta. I want to thank you for your loyalty and your business. I agree that all of these rules about where to smoke, when to smoke and what you can smoke are a little silly. However, the rules are made by the federal government, and I am charged with enforcing them."

He started to speak when I put up my hand to stop him.

"Before you and I get crossways on this, I think I have a solution that will satisfy us both. I have been addicted to nicotine myself in the past. I know life is unpleasant when you are deprived."

I pulled out the snuff. "Have you ever used this?"

"No, what is it?

"It's smokeless tobacco. In Texas, all the cowboys use it to get their nicotine and leave their hands free to rope calves. I am going to leave this with you. Just take a pinch and put it between your cheek and gum, and I guarantee you will get all the nicotine you want. The good part is nobody will be able to tell."

He agreed to try it, and I went back to the cockpit. I heard no more about this until after landing. The flight attendant said Mr. Tartan read for a while, then he looked out the window for a while, then he went to the lavatory for a long while. When he came out he looked pale. I now realized that I should have given him better instructions on using the Copenhagen. Beginners need a spit cup, and the pinch should be small. I am sure Mr. Tartan got plenty of nicotine.

To keep passenger goodwill, at times I forgave blatant violations. We were on the ground at the busy Chicago O'Hare airport. The controllers were in a slowdown due to a work dispute. We had been waiting for well over an hour to cross one runway. The passengers could see their terminal just on the other side, yet we could not get clearance to cross.

A flight attendant burst into the cockpit announcing that several passengers were about to open the emergency over-wing escape hatch and had stated they were going to the terminal.

I grabbed my hat and quickly proceeded to over-wing cabin area. There I saw the escape hatch already open and one 20-something male about to exit with another right behind him.

"WHOA, WHOA, guys you don't want to do this."

They looked at me and hesitated. One of them said, "I can see the terminal right there. We're tired of sitting here."

"Believe me, you do not want to do this. You will never make it to the terminal. If you don't get smashed by an airplane, you will be arrested and go to jail."

Sheepishly, they turned and gave up. I realized then they were half drunk. They had taken full advantage of free drinks I had authorized due to the inconvenience the delay was causing. I closed the hatch and after convincing them to sit, I returned to the cockpit. Although this was a flagrant violation with serious consequences, I let it go. Nothing else was said about the incident, and I'll bet their friends never believed the story.

It was a crisp fall day in New York City when I reported early for our scheduled limo pick up. I was standing outside the Park Sheraton hotel as a taxi arrived and the driver unloaded two bags for a well-dressed woman. She stepped out, turned to me and ordered, "Bring those bags to the check in desk."

She walked inside without so much as a backward glance. I looked around and decided she had to be talking to me. I picked up the two very heavy bags and lugged them inside to the desk. She turned and offered me a five dollar bill.

"No ma'am, that won't be necessary. Just come fly with us sometime."

It was only then that she realized she had mistaken my uniform.

Whether in daytime or the middle of the night, to cross the ocean or do a series of short hops, I always looked forward to work. I was doing what I loved, and I was with people I respected and liked. Delta referred to their employees as a family and, in some respects, it was. Every year, they were singled out as either the best company to work for, or the most admired company.

After I retired, the airline industry fell on hard times. Almost all the major carriers went through bankruptcy reorganization. Salaries were cut and benefits lost. Employee morale suffered. Today, that is behind Delta. It is once again on top and morale is climbing. Although much larger, the family is returning – *they love to fly and it shows.*

On my final airline trip, I had my last layover in Puerto Rico. When we departed the next morning on my last flight, the ground crew rolled out a paper sign that was 20 feet long. It said, "Happy retirement Capt. Taylor." I have no idea how they knew. On my final landing in Atlanta, fire trucks lined the ramp and made a giant water arch over our Lockheed L-1011. Inside the terminal, I was presented a large picture of an L-1011 with a border containing more than 200 signatures from crew members I had flown with. The picture on the cover of this book is me in the cockpit escape hatch at the gate in Atlanta after that final flight. I am waving as if I am happy, but in a close-up, you would see tears running down my face. That was one of the saddest days of my life.

THE END OF THE TRAIL

**STEVE TAYLOR** was raised on a farm in Mt. Pleasant, S.C. He graduated from Moultrie High School and is a 1960 graduate of The Citadel. He served six years as a pilot in the U.S. Air Force, with service in Vietnam. His long career as a Delta pilot, including international flying, occurred during the heyday of the jet age.

Taylor's reputation as a prankster is legendary. The stories contained herein could earn him a place in the Practical Jokers Hall of Fame, which currently doesn't exist. But it should.